Distant Horizons

Distant Horizons

Digital Evidence and Literary Change

TED UNDERWOOD

The University of Chicago Press ✳ Chicago and London

The University of Chicago Press, Chicago 60637
The University of Chicago Press, Ltd., London
© 2019 by The University of Chicago
Published 2019
Printed and bound by CPI Group (UK) Ltd, Croydon, CR0 4YY

28 27 26 25 24 23 22 21 20 19   1 2 3 4 5

ISBN-13: 978-0-226-61266-9 (cloth)
ISBN-13: 978-0-226-61283-6 (paper)
ISBN-13: 978-0-226-61297-3 (e-book)
DOI: https://doi.org/10.7208/chicago/9780226612973.001.0001

Library of Congress Cataloging-in-Publication Data

Names: Underwood, Ted, author.
Title: Distant horizons : digital evidence and literary change / Ted Underwood.
Description: Chicago : The University of Chicago Press, 2019. | Includes bibliographical references and index.
Identifiers: LCCN 2018036446 | ISBN 9780226612669 (cloth : alk. paper) | ISBN 9780226612836 (pbk. : alk. paper) | ISBN 9780226612973 (e-book)
Subjects: LCSH: Literature—Research—Methodology. | Digital humanities.
Classification: LCC PN73.U53 2019 | DDC 807.2—dc23
LC record available at https://lccn.loc.gov/2018036446

♾ This paper meets the requirements of ANSI/NISO Z39.48–1992 (Permanence of Paper).

Contents

Illustrations

Figures

Tables

Preface: The Curve of the Literary Horizon

This is a book about recent discoveries in literary history. The word *discovery* may sound odd, because the things that matter in literary history are usually arguments, not discoveries. Although lost manuscripts do occasionally turn up in an attic, uncovering new evidence is rarely the main purpose of literary research. Instead, scholars reinterpret the well-known outlines of the past (Romantic, Victorian, modern) by drawing new connections between texts or by moving something marginal to center stage.

Or so I thought ten years ago. Over the past decade, I have gradually lost confidence that the broad outlines of the literary past are as well known as I once thought. As scholars have learned to compare thousands of volumes at a time, we have stumbled onto broad, century-spanning trends that are not described in textbooks and not explained by period concepts. It is becoming clear that we have narrated literary history as a sequence of discrete movements and periods because chunks of that size are about as much of the past as a single person could remember and discuss at one time. Apparently, longer arcs of change have been hidden from us by their sheer scale—just as you can drive across a continent noticing mountains and political boundaries but never the curvature of the earth. A single pair of eyes at ground level can't grasp the curve of the horizon, and arguments limited by a single reader's memory can't reveal the largest patterns organizing literary history.

In this book, I explore some of those patterns and explain how new approaches to literary research are making them visible. I follow in the footsteps of many other scholars who have posed broad social questions about literature. The work described here owes something to twentieth-century projects like book history, stylistics, and the sociology of literature, as well as to the more recent fusion of those projects that goes under Franco Moretti's term "distant reading."[1] I will be less concerned to trace academic genealogies than to describe specific discoveries that are redrawing our map of the last three hundred years of English-language literature. The first four chapters are each organized around a different historical discovery—illuminating literary language, genre, aesthetic judgment, and the history of gender.

The book also describes the new methods required for large-scale research and discusses the reservations many people feel about applying computers to literature. But I do not approach those questions as they are commonly framed—as a struggle that pits critical tradition against a new technological initiative called "digital humanities." That frame has been popular for several reasons. It fits a familiar narrative that casts digital computers as the main agents of change in recent history, as well as an even older narrative organized around conflict between machines and culture. Well-worn stories of that kind come with a familiar set of moral coordinates, making it easy for observers to express an opinion about changes labeled "digital" without studying the changes themselves in much detail.

That's unfortunate, because the advances that have made large

---

1. For a long view of the interaction between these projects, see James F. English, "Everywhere and Nowhere: The Sociology of Literature after 'the Sociology of Literature,'" *New Literary History* 41, no. 2 (2010): v–xxiii.

historical patterns visible have less to do with computers than with new ideas about modeling and interpretation. Computers themselves, after all, are not very new; scholars have been applying them to literary language for more than fifty years. If digital technology had been the only thing required for a new approach to literary history, this book would have appeared long ago. But in the 1970s, the application of computers to literature often produced arguments about sentence length or about Jonathan Swift's favorite words. Most scholars doubted that a computer's ability to precisely measure those linguistic details would, in itself, transform the history of literary pleasure. In my view, they were right to be doubtful. As Stanley Fish pointed out, it's one thing to prove that Swift uses a lot of connective words and another to give that isolated fact a literary interpretation.[2]

So what changed over the last fifty years? Admittedly, scale is one part of the story. Up through the 1980s, quantitative exploration of literary history tended to be founded on relatively small collections, often focused on individual authors. The expansion of digital libraries has made it easier to pose broad historical questions, and historical breadth has given quantitative inquiry a better social foundation. (This book, for instance, is deeply indebted to HathiTrust Digital Library, among other sources.) But sheer scale is only part of the story. The discoveries described in this book do depend on a wide field of view—as the curve of the horizon only becomes visible some distance above the earth. But a wide field of view is not enough, by itself, to give linguistic details a literary meaning.

Numbers are becoming more useful in literary study for reasons that are theoretical rather than technical. It is not that computers got faster or disks got bigger but that we have recently graduated from measuring variables to framing models of literary

2. Stanley Fish, "What Is Stylistics, and Why Are They Saying Such Terrible Things About It?," in *Is There a Text in This Class? The Authority of Interpretive Communities* (Cambridge, MA: Harvard University Press, 1980), 68–96.

concepts.[3] Since a model defines a relationship between variables, a mode of inquiry founded on models can study relationships rather than isolated facts. Instead of starting with, say, the frequency of connective words, quantitative literary research now starts with social evidence about things that really interest readers of literature—like audience, genre, character, and gender. The literary meaning of those phenomena comes, in a familiar way, from historically grounded interpretive communities. Numbers enter the picture not as an objective foundation for meaning somewhere outside history but as a way to establish comparative relationships between different parts of the historical record.

I realize this is a loosely sketched picture. The word *model* itself is not yet common in literary study, so chapter 1 will spend some time explaining what it means to frame a statistical model (especially a "predictive model") of a literary concept. All I want to say at the outset is that the advances making this book possible were not mostly a matter of computing power. They have depended instead on a debate about modeling, learning, and interpretation that is currently transforming fields from statistics to psychology.[4]

I will dip into that debate throughout the book, and survey it more fully in an appendix on "Methods," in order to give readers a glimpse of important developments in recent intellectual history. But in the end, this is a book about the history of English literature, focusing especially on Anglo-American writers. Instead of emphasizing new methods, I will underline specific literary insights they make possible. Each chapter will be organized as a historical argument.

3. In foregrounding the concept of modeling, this book dovetails with several recent arguments on the same topic. Andrew Piper, "Think Small: On Literary Modeling," *PMLA* 132, no. 3 (2017): 651–58; Richard Jean So, "All Models Are Wrong," *PMLA* 132, no. 3 (2017): 668–73; Andrew Piper, *Enumerations: Data and Literary Study* (Chicago: University of Chicago Press, 2018), 9–12.

4. A full description of these debates will be deferred to appendix B. But see, for instance, Leo Breiman, "Statistical Modeling: The Two Cultures," *Statistical Science* 16, no. 3 (2001): 199–231; Tal Yarkoni and Jacob Westfall, "Choosing Prediction over Explanation in Psychology: Lessons from Machine Learning," *Perspectives on Psychological Science* 12, no. 6 (2017): 1100–22.

The first chapter suggests that many well-known changes in eighteenth-, nineteenth-, and twentieth-century fiction can be understood as parts of a single differentiating process that defined the subject, style, and pace of fiction through opposition to nonfiction. We already know about parts of this story. Scholars of eighteenth-century fiction have discussed the end of feigned autobiography, scholars of the nineteenth century talk about emphasis on visual detail, and scholars of modernism discuss the decline of the omniscient narrator.[5] From time to time, more controversially, a critic will suggest that some of these changes could be unified under the banner of a broader shift from "telling" toward "showing."[6] But it has been difficult to make a unified story persuasive: Victorians and postmodernists, for instance, may refuse to line up with modernist triumphalism about the rise of the impersonal, limited narrator.[7] With the broader perspective made possible by quantitative evidence, it is now possible to see all these changes as stages of a long differentiating process. A wide range of artistic movements, often said to conflict with each other, sometimes said to have sought rapprochement with "ordinary language," have all actually pushed fiction farther away from the language, themes, and narrative strategies of nonfiction.

Of course, "fiction" is a rather broad genre; literary scholars are more commonly interested in the history of subgenres like Gothic or detective fiction. Chapter 2 zooms in on those concepts in order to explain how new methods can support a perspectival approach to genre. The Aristotelian conception of genres as natural literary kinds has given way over the last fifty years to a warier approach that treats genres as historically contingent institutions. Instead of trying to give science fiction a stable definition, critics

5. Ian Watt, *The Rise of the Novel* (Berkeley: University of California Press, 1957), 297; Peter Brooks, *Realist Vision* (New Haven, CT: Yale University Press, 2005); Michael Levenson, *A Genealogy of Modernism: A Study of English Literary Doctrine 1908–1922* (Cambridge: Cambridge University Press, 1986), 8–9.

6. Percy Lubbock, *The Craft of Fiction* (1921; New York: Viking Press, 1957).

7. Wayne C. Booth, *The Rhetoric of Fiction* (Chicago: University of Chicago Press, 1964), 23–64.

increasingly propose that it is, at bottom, just the loose grouping of works that different historical actors have called "science fiction."[8] This implies that science fiction may have meant different things at different times and puts critics who want to talk about science fiction before the 1920s in an awkward position, since none of those literary traditions were called science fiction by their original readers.

Genres are not the only human creations that change their meanings with time. The interpretive problems that confront a history of genre are rooted in the perspectival dimension of history itself, and they run too deep to be solved neatly. The meaning of a term like *science fiction* will always depend on an observer's location. But one of the central arguments of this book is that contemporary quantitative methods can be very good at representing perspectival problems and can give us leverage on that dimension of history.

Questions of perspective may be the last place we would expect to encounter math. In the twentieth century, numbers were used mostly for physical measurements (or demographic counts) that didn't vary greatly from one observer to another. Those associations have given many people the impression that Arabic numbers are somehow in themselves objective or aspire to be independent of social context. But if we look with fresh eyes at contemporary quantitative methods, we may notice that they are not distinguished by any aspiration to objectivity. Machine learning, in particular, is causing public scandal because it tends to be all too sensitive to subjective contexts.

When scholars explicitly define a concept, we can craft a definition that aspires to neutrality. But the models produced by machine learning don't rely on explicit definitions; instead, they learn concepts entirely from illustrative examples. Learning from examples makes machine learning flexible but also very apt to pick up the assumptions or prejudices latent in a particular selec-

8. John Rieder, "On Defining SF, or Not: Genre Theory, SF, and History," *Science Fiction Studies* 37, no. 2 (2010): 191.

tion of evidence. This has become a huge problem for institutions that are expected to be neutral arbiters. We don't want a bank's judgments about creditworthiness to be shaped by assumptions about gender or race. But a model that learns about creditworthiness from examples of approved and rejected loans is very likely to absorb the biases of the people who approved or rejected them. Institutions that strive to be unbiased might well choose to avoid machine learning. When we're reasoning about the past, on the other hand, our aim is usually to acknowledge and explore biases, not to efface them. Understanding the subjective preferences implicit in a particular selection of literary works, for instance, may be exactly the goal of our research. For this kind of project, it is not a problem but a positive advantage that machine learning tends to absorb assumptions latent in the evidence it is trained on. By training models on evidence selected by different people, we can crystallize different social perspectives and compare them rigorously to each other.

This approach, which I call "perspectival modeling," has taken shape only in the last few years. Readers who are familiar with other ways of using machine learning may need to set some assumptions aside. The models created in this book are supervised: that is, they always start from evidence labeled by human readers. But unlike supervised models that try to divine the real author of an anonymous text, perspectival models do not aim simply to reproduce human judgment. They are used instead to measure the parallax between different observers.

This strategy will have many applications in the pages that follow. The second chapter, for instance, uses it to pose questions about the history of genre. In some cases, genres defined by observers in different periods turn out to align better than their names might suggest. A model trained on nineteenth-century "scientific romance" finds it easy to recognize contemporary "science fiction" as a version of the same thing. In other cases, different perspectives turn out to be incompatible: the various traditions readers have called "Gothic," for instance, aren't well recognized by a single model. Evidence like this can help historians move beyond sterile arguments about lumping and splitting and toward a more flexible debate that acknowledges boundaries with different degrees of blurriness.

Chapter 3 begins to explain how questions of form and genre intersect with grittier aspects of literary production and distribution. This requires enriching a library of texts with social context—so we know, for instance, which works became commercial successes or critical favorites. Armed with that evidence, scholars can ask how literary trends were related to the pressures exerted by the marketplace or by changing patterns of critical judgment. This inquiry reveals a strikingly regular pattern, where the criteria defining literary prominence align strongly with directions of change across long periods of time. The arc of literary history is long, but it bends (so to speak) toward prestige. At this point, we are no longer simply transforming familiar accounts of history by backing up to take a longer view of them. If standards of aesthetic judgment have remained relatively stable for centuries at a time, and have shaped literary change over equally long timelines, then we are looking at an account of literary history that is basically at odds with the story of rapid generational reversal told in our textbooks and anthologies.

The first three chapters of the book describe dimensions of literary history (like reception and genre) where volumes can be discussed for the most part as wholes. Topics like plot and character are harder to trace across long timelines because they require divisions below the volume level that are challenging to tease out algorithmically. But with collaborative support from computer scientists, it is also possible to make some progress on those topics. Chapter 4 explores the history of characterization, looking in particular at the way fictional characters are shaped by implicit assumptions about gender. Once again, perspectival models provide crucial leverage for my argument. For instance, one way to ask how strongly characterization has been gendered is to ask how easy it would be to distinguish fictional women from men, using only the things they are represented as doing in the text. When first names and pronouns are set aside, can a model still predict a character's grammatical gender? And if so, how do perspectives on gender vary across time? Using tools built in part by David Bamman, I have been able to show that the implicit gendering of character grows steadily blurrier from 1840 to the present. More interesting, of course, are the specific details that signify gender. These are not always obvious: in the middle of the twentieth century, it suddenly becomes feminine to smile but masculine to grin. Perhaps most interesting of all: the details that predict a character's gender turn out to be extremely volatile. Fictive gender is not the same thing today that it was in 1840. Along the way, we'll stumble over some counterintuitive trends in the social history of authorship—notably, a 50% decline in the fraction of English-language fiction written by women between 1850 and 1970.

The approach to literary history I have outlined above is controversial, to say the least. Literary arguments don't ordinarily use numbers, and many scholars doubt that numbers can ever play an important role in the humanities. The fifth chapter of this book responds to those concerns in depth.

I delay this controversy to the end of the book because I don't see it as a struggle between competing philosophies that could be decided in advance by invoking first principles. Doubts about the value of large-scale quantitative research are doubts about the inherent interest of a new perspective on the past, and there is simply no way to know whether a new perspective will be interesting until you have explored it. At the end of this book, after exploring a new scale of description, I will weigh its inherent interest against the price humanists might have to pay for this expansion of their horizons.

There is, to be sure, a price to be paid for all knowledge. But in this case, the price is institutional rather than philosophical. We are not looking at a debate like the struggle between structuralism and poststructuralism, where one perspective had to be abandoned in order to adopt another. Distant reading is simply a new scale of description. It doesn't conflict with close reading any more than an anatomical diagram of your hand would conflict with the chemical reactions going on inside your cells. Instead of displacing previous scales of literary description, distant reading has the potential to expand the discipline—rather as biochemistry expanded chemistry toward a larger scale of analysis. And yet there is admittedly a cost, even to expansion: new kinds of training could stretch scholars and perhaps change the character of a literature department. So in the fifth chapter, I meditate on the temperament and training required for quantitative research in the humanities and let readers decide whether the new perspective unfolded in the first four chapters would be worth paying the associated price.

But costs can only be weighed against benefits after we see what long timelines reveal. The most I can achieve in a preface is to clear up a few misunderstandings that might scare readers away at the outset. One concern, in particular, may spring to mind the moment you open this book and see a graph: that quantitative methods seek to strip away the interpretive dimension of the humanities in order to produce objective knowledge.

This notion springs, I think, from a failure of communication between humanists and scientists. To make a long story short: numbers are not inherently more or less objective than words. Numbers are just signs created by human beings to help us reason about questions of degree. Like other arguments about the past, a statistical model is a tentative interpretation of evidence. Expressing a model mathematically has the advantage of making some assumptions explicit (including, especially, assumptions about quantity and degree). But numbers have no special power to settle questions: assumptions and inferences still have to be hammered out through a familiar process of debate. In literary history, moreover, scholars will often be using statistics to model aspects of the world that are themselves subjective beliefs. In exploring genre, for instance, I have modeled variables like "the probability that a particular group of observers in 1973 would have *thought* this was an example of detective fiction."

In other words, a quantitative approach to literature does not have to be premised on a belief that literary history is governed by any drily factual Marxist or Darwinian logic. While this book sketches patterns of change across long timelines, it will generally resist the assumption that literary history can be explained by a familiar master narrative. The first chapter of this book will begin where readers of literature usually begin—by exploring the details of two particular stories. As we back up, it is true, those details will start to organize themselves into larger patterns shared by many other books. And in an attempt to understand those patterns, we will start to form generalizations we call models. Those models will reveal large patterns that scholars have previously failed to describe. But they won't eliminate perspectival differences and debate. Quantitative models are no more objective than any other historical interpretation; they are just another way to grapple with the mystery of the human past, which doesn't become less complex or less perplexing as we back up to take a wider view.

The second set of misunderstandings I want to address at the outset involves a polemical definition of "distant reading" that Franco Moretti advanced about nineteen years ago. I have embraced the term "distant reading" because it is apt, and because I am wary of the academic tendency to simultaneously disavow and appropriate the past by rebranding it. ("Everyone knows that distant reading was naïve, but I have invented *critical* distant reading, which is quite another matter!") Endless rebranding is tiresome. However, it needs to be said that the way to evaluate distant reading, in 2019, is to look at the results recently produced by a growing community of scholars—not to stage a debate with a speculative rationale for this project that Franco Moretti put forward in the year 2000.

Moretti was not the first scholar to propose exploring the literary past with social-scientific methods and digital texts. Similar projects, inflected by corpus linguistics, sociology, and book history, were already under way in the 1980s and 1990s.[9] The project accelerated dramatically at the beginning of this century, fueled

9. Janice Radway, *Reading the Romance: Women, Patriarchy, and Popular Literature* (Chapel Hill: University of North Carolina Press, 1984); Mark Olsen, "Signs, Symbols, and Discourses: A New Direction for Computer-Aided Literary Studies," *Computers and the Humanities* 27 (1993/1994): 309–14.

by a set of social and conceptual innovations that could support large-scale research (digital libraries, for instance, and machine learning). But few of those factors were visible to most literary scholars in the year 2000. Instead, distant reading was initially understood as an extension of the canon-expanding recovery projects of the 1990s. This gave the enterprise a moral claim on scholars' attention. If you didn't do distant reading, you were presumably ignoring the cries of thousands of volumes forgotten in "the slaughterhouse of literature."[10]

Nineteen years later, the project of large-scale literary history is still often called distant reading because the phrase is vivid and appropriate. But the project has outgrown the polemics that originally accompanied its name. For instance, Moretti's emphasis on the moral urgency of recovery prompted many skeptics to reply that digital libraries themselves still exclude many volumes that are either lost or simply not digitized. No collection, however large, can save every work from the slaughterhouse.[11] This is true. It is also not an objection to contemporary practices of distant reading, which usually work with explicitly limited samples. The point of distant reading is not to recover a complete archive of all published works but to understand the contrast between samples drawn from different periods or social contexts.

In this and many other ways, distant readers and their critics are often simply talking past each other. Quantitative approaches to literary history have been quite productive, but the results they have produced are not the results predicted by their most notorious manifestoes. The differences between the canon and the slaughterhouse, for instance, turn out not to be enormous. Prominent and obscure writers are often moving in roughly the same direction.[12] But in expanding the scope of their analyses, distant

10. Franco Moretti, "The Slaughterhouse of Literature," *Modern Language Quarterly* 61, no. 1 (2000): 207–27.

11. Amanda Gailey, "Some Big Problems with Big Data," *American Periodicals: A Journal of History and Criticism* 26, no. 1 (2016): 22–24.

12. Mark Algee-Hewitt, Sarah Allison, Marissa Gemma, Ryan Heuser, Franco Moretti, and Hannah Walser, "Canon/Archive. Large-Scale Dynamics in the Literary Field," Stanford Literary Lab, January 2016, https://litlab.stanford.edu/LiteraryLabPamphlet11.pdf.

readers have stumbled onto long historical arcs that change what we thought we knew about both groups of writers, canonical and obscure.

It is time for this conversation to refocus. Distant readers need new manifestoes that provoke critics to respond to what they have actually done—which might be even more interesting than what they had promised to do two decades ago. This book refocuses the conversation in one of several possible ways, by shifting emphasis from sheer archival comprehensiveness to the sweep of long timelines.

The methods I will be describing do, of course, have limits. It would be a mistake to push numbers into every corner of literary study merely because they are new and fun. Critics who want to sensitively describe the merits of a single work usually have no need for statistics. Enthusiasm for computers and glossy pictures has sometimes led observers to overstate how much can be added to our understanding of a single book by, say, network graphs detailing the connections between its characters. Computational analysis of text is more flexible than it used to be, but it is still quite crude compared to human reading; it helps mainly with questions where the evidence is simply too big to fit in a single reader's memory. This is why quantitative methods have contributed especially to our understanding of long timelines.

On the other hand, a book about literary history cannot spend all its time thirty thousand feet above the ground. Literature grips readers through individual characters and resonant details; literary history needs to do the same thing. This is especially true for a history of modern literature. As chapters 1 and 3 explain, concrete specificity has become steadily more important to poetry and fiction across the last three hundred years and constitutes at present the main stylistic difference separating literary genres from nonfiction. A history of modern literature that confined itself to sweeping generalization would fail to convey a crucial dimension of its subject. So, while taking a very wide view of history, this book does also plunge into case studies of individual authors and close readings of selected passages.

The rhetorical and aesthetic strains created by this juxtaposition of scales pose the real challenge for distant reading. There may be no conflict, in principle, between quantitative reasoning and humanistic interpretation. But it remains true that literary scholarship aims at an aesthetic standard more exacting than the one prevailing in science. Can distant readers write quantitative literary history that is nevertheless detailed enough, streamlined enough, and lively enough to interest a wide range of readers? If we can't, then no argument will save us: what we are doing may be important, but it will belong in the social sciences. I hope to show that numbers can also be at home in the humanities. But I cannot prove that in advance. I can only aspire to demonstrate it by writing a book that uses statistical models to tell a suspenseful story of broad human interest.

1

Do We Understand the Outlines
of Literary History?

Literary studies is littered with terms that suggest one critical practice has displaced another: poststructuralism, postmodernism, New Criticism, New Historicism. Even "distant reading" is often understood as a would-be successor to "close reading." Habits of debate are by no means a bad thing: they make conversation in an English department playful and agile. But it is worth teasing out the assumptions implied by these succession stories—which are not dominant, after all, in every corner of the university. Many disciplines tell their own stories instead as a cumulative process of expansion. Bioinformatics has not replaced biochemistry. Although these different approaches to the study of life admittedly compete for resources, no one imagines that the exchanges between them are zero-sum games or that one has displaced the other.

Literary scholars, by contrast, commonly do assume that critical approaches are locked in dialectical struggle. And this assumption is not arbitrary: the premise has been correct for much of our history. Critical debates amount to struggles over a scarce resource—readerly attention. Should the ghosts in *The Turn of the Screw* be experienced as repressed desires or as a suppressed class identity? We can say both, but dividing classroom time between interpretations is still a zero-sum problem. Even when scholars move from theoretical debate to archival research, our enterprise seems to draw meaning from the pressure of limited attention: recovery projects become notable and important (rather than merely additive) when they argue that new discoveries force us to redefine an established concept like Romanticism.

I'm dwelling on these disciplinary habits in order to highlight the assumption on which they all rest. Literary scholars tend to feel they are arguing about the redistribution of interpretive emphasis within fixed historical outlines. Implicit in this self-understanding is an assumption that the broad divisions of literary debate are already known: that we are unlikely to discover, for instance, a new genre or period in the archives. It seems a safe assumption, because the historical organization of our discipline has been relatively stable, compared to the list of research topics in biology. There are exceptions—especially toward the contemporary end of the timeline, where new terms are always taking shape. But once a list of periods, movements, and genres has consolidated, it tends to endure: if you page through old college catalogs, you find courses on "Elizabethan Drama" and "English Romanticism" offered in unbroken succession from 1900 to the present.[1] Nor is it clear yet that distant reading has altered the logic of this game. Franco Moretti's "Slaughterhouse of Literature," for instance, could be read as a new approach to a familiar topic. Although Moretti gestures at a mass of unread works, literary scholars have been reluctant to believe that this really creates a new object of knowledge, seeing instead a familiar dialectical move that plants a new flag on terrain of recognized significance (say, detective fiction) by claiming to displace a critical approach called close reading.[2]

1. Ted Underwood, *Why Literary Periods Mattered: Historical Contrast and the Prestige of English Studies* (Stanford, CA: Stanford University Press, 2013), 114.

2. Moretti, "Slaughterhouse." Distant reading is so rarely interpreted as multiplying objects of study, and so commonly interpreted as an attempted displacement of close reading, that examples are almost superfluous—but take, for instance, Joseph North, *Literary Criticism: A Concise Political History* (Cambridge, MA: Harvard University Press, 2017), 111–15. One can admittedly find passages in Moretti to justify the interpretation.

This model of disciplinary history was well founded in the twentieth century. But I would argue that it is unreliable today. Distant reading may have begun by proposing to displace existing approaches to detective fiction and the nineteenth-century novel, but it is turning out to matter in a less familiar way: by uncovering new objects of knowledge. As literary historians stumble over a growing number of trends that span two or three centuries, we are beginning to realize that we moved too hastily in assuming that our discipline had been mapped, or even loosely sketched. Do we actually understand the broad outlines of literary history? I think we understand them well at a generational scale, and hazily at the level of a single century. But as we back up farther, the limits of our knowledge become evident: large patterns emerge for which we don't yet have names.

Moreover, these historical patterns are not alternatives to the canon: they are broad trends that embrace Jane Austen and Toni Morrison along with the "great unread."[3] Discoveries of this kind don't create yet another approach to *The Turn of the Screw*; they occupy a different scale of historical description and require a different kind of debate. Literary historians will still have plenty to argue about, since large frames do change our understanding of the things inside them. But the specific martial talents we developed in fights over anthologies and critical editions become a bit beside the point here. Instead of staging normative arguments about the right approach to a limited number of familiar topics, we need to explore ways of coordinating different scales of analysis.

The Horizon of Literary Knowledge

For instance, this chapter about our ignorance of long-term trends might begin by acknowledging how much we already know at a local level. To show off our achievements, we could choose a task that literary scholars have spent some time practicing—say, the

3. Margaret Cohen, *The Sentimental Education of the Novel* (Princeton, NJ: Princeton University Press, 1999), 23.

explication of short passages in novels. Here are two versions of
a situation that has been common in fiction: in both, two young
people are developing a romantic attachment, without full awareness of the attachment yet on either side. How much literary
history can we extract from the contrast between the passages?

> Sophia, with the highest degree of innocence and modesty, had a
> remarkable degree of sprightliness in her temper. This was so greatly
> increased whenever she was in company with Tom, that had he not
> been very young and thoughtless, he must have observed it; or had
> not Mr. Western's thoughts been generally either in the field, the
> stable, or the dog-kennel, it might perhaps have created some jeal-
> ousy in him: but so far was the good gentleman from entertaining
> any such suspicion, that he gave Tom every opportunity with his
> daughter that any lover could have wished; and this Tom innocently
> improved to better advantage, by following only the dictates of his
> natural gallantry and good-nature, than he might perhaps have done
> had he had the deepest designs on the young lady.[4]

This passage is not difficult to date—first of all, because many
readers will recognize Sophia Western as a character from *The
History of Tom Jones* (1749). But even readers unfamiliar with that
book may guess that they're listening to an eighteenth-century
voice. Qualities like modesty and good nature are confidently attributed to characters in long sentences articulated by wry counterfactual conditions. The narrator is so casually omniscient, in
fact, that he can call his protagonist "very young and thoughtless"
in passing. The second passage is almost equally easy to place on
a timeline, although very few people alive today are likely to have
read this novel.

> The last time he had been in a boat with a girl, it had been Aileen
> who had sat in the bow against a background of sparkling sea and
> deep blue sky, and in her scarlet cap, the young gull's wing he had
> given her. Now against a background of green branches and sun-
> flecked water there sat opposite him a gray-eyed young woman of

4. Henry Fielding, *The History of Tom Jones, a Foundling* (New York: Modern Library, 1950), 119–20.

whom at first he had been a little afraid. But facing her half-wearied quiet, and remembering the shadow picture of ten days before, he felt much more at his ease. "And the little breeze? Y're catching it?" he said. He could see that it had caught her, for it was blowing the soft hair around her ears and lifting the ends of her black four-in-hand tie.

"Oh, yes! And it is delicious! It is much nicer even than—than soy beans!"[5]

Like *Tom Jones*, this story of growing affection has a rural setting, and both passages even develop a brief comic sidelight involving a character distracted from love by agriculture. But readers will have little difficulty discerning that the passages are separated by more than a century.

What gives the second passage away is an elaborate strategy of indirection. Readers are not told that Patrick Joyce is beginning to love Olivia Ladd—only that he notices her "half-wearied quiet" and the motion of the "soft hair around her ears." But we also know that his feelings are divided, because her image is juxtaposed with the image of another woman. The divided feelings seem intense. How else should we interpret the strange vividness of these images? The contrast between women requires four color adjectives in the space of two sentences—deep blue, scarlet, green, gray—followed shortly by a fifth, when Patrick notices Olivia's black tie. This rigorous insistence on expressing emotions indirectly by tracing a character's flickering attentiveness to physical sensations probably tells us that we're somewhere near the early twentieth century, although, as it happens, Frances Allen published *The Invaders* in 1913, six years before T. S. Eliot popularized the phrase "objective correlative."[6]

Works of fiction from different periods invite readers to play very different interpretive games. We might not even need formal training in literary history to feel the differences and place

5. Frances Newton Symmes Allen, *The Invaders* (Boston: Houghton Mifflin, 1913), 151–52.

6. Allen, *The Invaders*; T. S. Eliot, *The Sacred Wood: Essays on Poetry and Criticism* (London: Methuen, 1920), 92.

the passages on a timeline. Where readers do have historical training, it becomes fair to ask harder questions—for instance, Why are these passages so different? Since the author of the first is famous, it will be tempting to answer the question there by invoking common knowledge about Henry Fielding: his narrators are comically intrusive and opinionated even for the eighteenth century. I have chosen the second passage from a little-known author to prevent us from leaning entirely on that kind of personal explanation. Although she published three novels that were well regarded at the time, Frances Allen is discussed today mainly in local histories of Deerfield, Massachusetts.[7] When it is remembered at all, *The Invaders* is remembered for exploring tensions around immigration: Patrick Joyce is "a little afraid" of Olivia Ladd in part because her family is hostile to the Irish, who (along with the Polish) are the invaders of the title. But little has been said about Allen's aesthetic choices. If we want to set her in a literary frame, we will have to back out at least to the level of the period. Henry James might provide one precedent for her tactic of limiting third-person narration to a particular character's perceptions. Allen doesn't stick to a single character's perspective as consistently as James, but she was one of hundreds of turn-of-the-century writers who discovered that focusing description on physical sensations and objects could, paradoxically, dramatize their characters' subjectivity.

Anyone with a degree in English could write paragraphs like the last three above, which characterize both passages, and situate them in the context of a period. This is the kind of thing we're good at. But if we back out a bit farther and try to draw a single line all the way from Henry Fielding to Frances Allen, we enter a scale of description where literary history becomes speculative at best. To be sure, there are stories in circulation we could lean on. For instance, one "critical tradition," according to Paul Dawson,

7. Michael C. Batinski, *Pastkeepers in a Small Place: Five Centuries in Deerfield, Massachusetts* (Amherst: University of Massachusetts Press, 2004), 206–7.

"favours a historical view of the novel progressing towards an invisible narrator who will simply present events (or experience) without commentary or evaluation."[8] It's a view of history often mixed up with a normative opinion that good writers "show" stories instead of "telling" them. Fielding was certainly a teller, and Allen's tactic of expressing human feeling through colors and wind-ruffled hair qualifies as an extreme form of showing. So these passages fit the alleged historical pattern.

But frankly, I chose both passages for that reason. How confident are we that the rest of literary history between 1749 and 1913 can be organized around a transition from telling to showing? There are critics who have implied a version of that argument. Percy Lubbock and F. R. Leavis are well-known examples.[9] But it would be an understatement to say that their interpretation of history remains controversial. Other scholars have pointed out that Leavis's grand narrative about the rise of impersonal narration forces him to underrate George Eliot, and even Joseph Conrad.[10] It is clear that limited third-person perspective had a good run from Henry James through Virginia Woolf but not at all clear that previous nineteenth-century fiction should be understood as a slow progress in that direction. Omniscient exposition permitted the characteristic strengths of the Victorian novel, and it remains important today in postmodern metafiction and genre fiction.[11] The once-dominant historical narrative about the rise of impersonal "showing" now looks suspiciously like a Whig history constructed by modernists to glorify a particular modernist practice. Many literary historians have followed Wayne Booth's

8. Paul Dawson, *Creative Writing and the New Humanities* (New York: Routledge, 2005), 103.

9. Lubbock, *Craft of Fiction*; F. R. Leavis, *The Great Tradition: George Eliot, Henry James, Joseph Conrad* (New York: George W. Stewart, [1950]).

10. Eleanor Courtemanche, *The "Invisible Hand" and British Fiction, 1818–1860: Adam Smith, Political Economy, and the Genre of Realism* (Houndmills: Palgrave, 2011), 186–87; Dawson, *Creative Writing*, 104.

11. Paul Dawson, *The Return of the Omniscient Narrator: Authorship and Authority in Twenty-First-Century Fiction* (Columbus: Ohio State University Press, 2015).

lead in replacing it with a more complex ecology of rhetorical techniques.[12]

In short, literary-historical knowledge is extremely rich within certain chronological limits. We are good at using short passages to characterize authors, movements, and periods. But if we try to stitch those pictures together to map a longer timeline, consensus becomes elusive.[13] Scholars have certainly tried to make century-spanning arguments. But it's hard to stage a focused debate about critical generalizations on this scale, since every reader frames the pattern at issue slightly differently and sees different writers as exemplary. Historians who think highly of modernism, or of Henry James, are more likely to believe in a broad shift from "telling" toward "showing" than historians who think highly of postmodernism or George Eliot. Scholars do agree about some simple long-term trends: the decline of rhymed poetry, for instance. Beyond that, we have influential hypotheses and long-running debates. But in contexts where we need consensus (like a classroom anthology), historical generalizations are typically limited to periods.

Nor is this limitation necessarily perceived as a problem. Since our disciplinary institutions are also built around periods, literary scholars specializing in different centuries are rarely forced to reach agreement about long-term patterns. Disagreements between historical fields often present themselves as normal, even inevitable temperamental differences between people who have chosen to study different things. So we let the argument drop and move on to something else. It's not obvious that these debates could ever be resolved simply by discussing a larger number of books.

12. Booth, *Rhetoric of Fiction*, 23–64.

13. The image of a "long timeline" will be in many ways central to the argument of this book. Other ways of imagining time are possible—and, one might argue, currently dominant in literary study. Instead of an even line, for instance, we could postulate a sequence of "periods" punctuated by revolutionary transformations. I don't argue that the linear metaphor is superior, only that it can reveal patterns we have not yet described. For the history of the timeline itself, see Daniel Rosenberg and Anthony Grafton, *Cartographies of Time: A History of the Timeline* (Princeton, NJ: Princeton Architectural, 2012).

Measurement

And in fact, I don't recommend trying to resolve a dizzying argument like the one between Percy Lubbock and Wayne Booth simply by multiplying examples. It is often more useful to reframe the question as we back up to consider a longer timeline. For instance, what happens if we bracket this sprawling debate about narratorial impersonality and "showing" in order to focus on some apparently trivial descriptive detail?

Take the names of colors. I may not have persuaded you that they signal emotion in the passage I quoted from *The Invaders*, but there is no denying that colors are oddly prominent in that book and comparatively absent in Fielding. Could that difference reflect, by any chance, a broader shift in the language of fiction?

Color perception may seem a basic constant in human experience, but its role in fiction has changed rather dramatically, as we see in figure 1.1. There is, to be sure, a lot of variation from one volume to another; most early-twentieth-century novelists were not as obsessed with visual experience as Frances Allen. (The fact that she and her sister both lost their hearing and worked as photographers is possibly relevant.) But the rising significance of color is not a personal idiosyncrasy; in fact, references to color are about three times more common, on average, in early-twentieth-century fiction than they had been in the eighteenth century. (Here, I am describing changes in the central trend line in figure 1.1, which reflects a mean value for the volumes plotted; we can have 95% confidence that the real trend falls somewhere in the shaded area at any given point on the timeline.) The meaning of this trend is not immediately legible. But the evidence itself is clear, and robust enough to resist two familiar forms of skepticism.

For instance, it is true that the concept of color has blurry boundaries. The list of words I have counted here is long enough to include colors like "cerulean," but there will always be chromatic experiences it leaves out and emotions that it mistakes for a color when tallying up occurrences of a word like "blue." If we

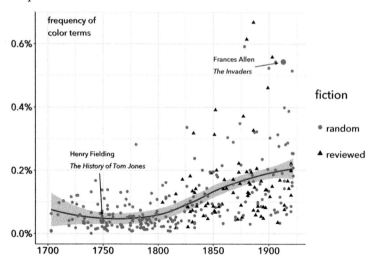

FIGURE 1.1. Frequency of color terms in a random sample of fiction, 1700–1922. Points represent 347 individual volumes. After 1800, volumes reviewed in a sample of prestigious magazines are distinguished as black triangles.

were looking specifically at the history of "blue," the rise and fall of its various senses might be crucial. But the rising frequency of reference to color in fiction is not driven by the expansion of any single term: all the primary colors become more common together, in parallel. Semantic nuances won't explain away this trend.

A second obvious form of skepticism involves questions about the particular sample of works discussed in figure 1.1. Questions of this kind can be important. In fact, as we'll see in chapter 3, a great deal can be learned by paying attention to the subtle differences between literary texts sampled in different ways— drawn from reviews in prestigious journals, say, or from the obscure reaches of an academic library. But it is also important to grasp that the subtle differences between samples rarely make a century-spanning trend disappear. Figure 1.1 covers 347 volumes of fiction, sampled from HathiTrust Digital Library using methods described in appendix A. But I have also divided the volumes after 1800 into two subsets, highlighting those that I found reviewed in selective Anglo-American literary magazines. References to color after 1800 may be just slightly more common in these prominent volumes than in contemporaneous, relatively obscure works. But the difference is faint; the trend won't change direction depending on the group we select.

Here, the prominence of Franco Moretti's speculative rationale for distant reading may have created misleading expectations. Moretti hypothesized that the "slaughterhouse" of forgotten works might contain a history very different from the one preserved in academic canons. Some readers naturally replied that canonical works "for better or worse . . . have achieved a position of cultural centrality" and ought to have more weight in our histories.[14] Because the topic of canonicity is charged with passion left over from twentieth-century cultural warfare, this debate caught fire before either side had carefully weighed the difference it made. Across long timelines, it turns out not to make much. On many axes of measurement, prominent and obscure writers are traveling together in the same direction, albeit at slightly (and interestingly) different speeds.[15] The trends we perceive in the slaughterhouse are usually also visible in the canon. While it is worth exploring the differences between samples, we don't have to reach consensus on a correctly balanced list of works before beginning to map long-term trends. (And that is of course fortunate, since there may be no single correctly balanced list.)

But have we actually begun to understand this trend yet? The rising frequency of color words is an intriguing clue but not an immediately legible one. We could make up plausible explanations—new dyes derived from coal tar, the rise of consumer culture, a vast phenomenological shift toward visual experience. Or we could look at the two passages I have already quoted and infer (with a doubtful shrug) that maybe the rising prominence of color in fiction somehow reflects the decline of

14. Moretti, "Slaughterhouse," 207–9; Jeremy Rosen, "Combining Close and Distant, or the Utility of Genre Analysis," *Post45* (December 3, 2011), http://post45.research.yale .edu/2011/12/combining-close-and-distant-or-the-utility-of-genre-analysis-a-response -to-matthew-wilkens-contemporary-fiction-by-the-numbers/.

15. Algee-Hewitt et al., "Canon/Archive," 6.

omniscient third-person narration. But the truth is that we don't understand what happened yet.

One way to tease out a better explanation is to look for other trends that correlate with this one. Correlation doesn't prove causation, as we have all learned to say, but the tests that do prove causation (like controlled experiments) are hard to apply to the historical record. Moreover, our understanding of history is often so sketchy that things far short of a causal explanation can improve it substantially. In this case, for instance, it would be interesting to know whether other words used in concrete physical description were also increasing in frequency. If they were, we might say that the rising prominence of color was part of a broader trend—which would enrich our description of this phenomenon, even if it doesn't explain it causally.

This is a question that literary scholars have recently addressed. In 2012, a pair of graduate students at Stanford (Ryan Heuser and Long Le-Khac) published a pamphlet pointing out that the rising frequency of concrete adjectives in nineteenth-century novels does indeed correlate with the rising prominence of colors, names of body parts, action verbs, and other words used in physical description. (The authors call this group of words "hard seeds," because the rising frequency of the word "hard" was the first clue they stumbled on.) While these categories were taking up more space in novels, another set of words they designate "abstract values" steadily dwindled in frequency. Heuser and Le-Khac conclude that nineteenth-century fictional discourse was transitioning "from telling to showing"—from directly expressed social judgment to judgment indirectly evoked through physical detail. They connect this shift speculatively to urbanization and "the less knowable community of urban social spaces."[16]

This thesis may sound more familiar than it is. The transition from telling to showing is a well-worn theme in literary history, as we have seen, but it has most commonly been traced through

16. Ryan Heuser and Long Le-Khac, "A Quantitative Literary History of 2,958 British Novels: The Semantic Cohort Method," Stanford Literary Lab Pamphlet 4, May 2012, http://litlab.stanford.edu/LiteraryLabPamphlet4.pdf, 45, 43.

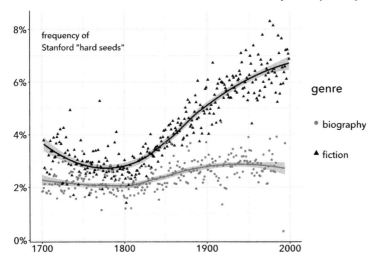

FIGURE 1.2. Frequency of Stanford "hard seeds" as percentage of fiction and biography. Data points represent yearly averages for each genre.

late-nineteenth- and early-twentieth-century examples: writers like Flaubert and James, Conrad and Woolf, who experiment with point of view. By shifting attention from narrative perspective to a looser index of physical description, Heuser and Le-Khac profoundly change the meaning of this theme: their version of "showing" is no longer quite what Percy Lubbock meant by celebrating Flaubert's impersonality.[17] But they also create a broader, longer story: the transformation they are tracing is already well under way in 1800.

It is possible to broaden their story even further. Using volumes drawn from HathiTrust Digital Library and ECCO-TCP, we can stretch Heuser and Le-Khac's nineteenth-century timeline for a century on either side, so it runs from 1700 to 2000.[18] To make the story more interesting, we can also add nonfictional biographies (and autobiographies) as a contrastive touchstone. In figure 1.2, I have plotted the proportion of the words that

17. Lubbock, *Craft of Fiction*, 59–92.

18. Eighteenth-Century Collections Online: Text Creation Partnership, accessed June 2, 2018, https://quod.lib.umich.edu/e/ecco/.

belong to Heuser and Le-Khac's "hard seeds" in 3,821 volumes (aggregated by year). One can see that the trend they traced in the nineteenth century continues straight through the twentieth. On the other hand, it doesn't extrapolate indefinitely into the past; as we move back into the early eighteenth century, the trend reverses and diction starts to become more concrete. Most interesting of all, this was not a broad transformation of the English language affecting all genres to the same degree. Instead, emphasis on physical description creates a gap between fiction and nonfiction—a difference that has steadily increased over the course of the last two centuries.

If figure 1.2 holds up to examination, it will already answer the question in the title of this chapter. It appears there are at least a few broad trends in literary history that we don't yet understand. For instance, our initial description of a passage from *The Invaders* certainly noticed that it was more vividly physical than *Tom Jones*, but critical tradition led us to connect that difference to recent innovations by James, or to the "objective correlative" Eliot would define a few years later. It was not immediately clear that the shift at issue could be extrapolated back to the late eighteenth century and forward to the late twentieth. If I had said, "Frances Allen's insistence on physical description dramatizes a transformation of fiction that continued steadily from 1780 to 2000 and places her well ahead of the curve for 1913," readers would rightly have laughed at my arbitrary assertion. That isn't necessarily a counterintuitive story: it may, in retrospect, be a plausible one. But the fact that something is retrospectively plausible doesn't mean we already knew it.

In fact, this account of literary history is so far from being self-evident that readers may not yet be persuaded. Heuser and Le-Khac make an appealing connection to social history by positing that "the less knowable community of urban social spaces" required a less judgmental descriptive mode limited to physical detail. But this explanation doesn't hold up well when we broaden our perspective beyond the nineteenth-century novel. It is strange, for instance, that the trend toward physical description falls from 1700 to 1780 and then starts rising. Did urban communities somehow become *more* knowable from 1700 to 1780? London was already growing in size. Even more puzzling: Why should urbanization have exerted such radically different effects on fictional and nonfictional narratives from 1780 forward? We might reply that novelists had to describe the experienced texture of life, while biographers could continue to rely on broad summary. But the novel's growing insistence on experienced detail is the phenomenon we're trying to explain. We can't take it for granted in our explanation.

A deeper problem is that it becomes difficult to get interpretive leverage on a trend defined purely through lists of words. A list of colors may not be too controversial: English contains a finite number of common color terms. The boundaries of the concept can get blurry (is *iridescence* the name of a color?), but this blurriness around the margins won't profoundly alter the aggregate trend. The same thing cannot be said of a category like "physical description." It would be impossible to list everything physical in the world. More crucially, once we start listing words associated with a category this broad, it is hard to know where to stop.

For instance, we can compare the Stanford hard seeds to semantic categories created fifty years ago to support textual analysis and preserved as the Harvard General Inquirer.[19] If we combine the lists of words that the General Inquirer tags as "descriptive action verbs," "spatial relationships," "body parts," and "colors," we get a subset of vocabulary that rises in almost exactly the same way as the lists constructed by the Stanford researchers (the two lists have 87% of their variance across volumes in common). So the problem is not that lists of words are simply idiosyncratic or arbitrary. Lists of action verbs constructed by different hands do tend to behave the same way. But there are

19. Roger Hurtwitz, General Inquirer Home Page, accessed April 27, 2016, http://www.wjh.harvard.edu/~inquirer/Home.html; Philip J. Stone, Dexter C. Dunphy, Marshall S. Smith, and Daniel M. Ogilvie, *The General Inquirer: A Computer Approach to Content Analysis* (Cambridge, MA: MIT Press, 1966).

also less strictly physical categories in the General Inquirer that rise across the timeline of fiction in much the same way as the ones listed above: for instance, verbs of perception (*see, hear*) and references to time (*quickly, moment, waited*). Characterizing this whole trend as a shift from abstract values to concrete description feels incomplete. It might be more satisfying to call it a shift toward description of immediate experience—toward the detailed narration of events that critics call "scene" rather than "summary."

I'm not suggesting that the lists of words in the General Inquirer are somehow better than those developed at Stanford. My point is rather that all semantic categories are imperfect, and no list of categories (however flexible) will provide a secure foundation for literary-historical inquiry. We can list the names of colors, and perhaps action verbs, but there will always be concepts like "temporal immediacy" that escape our preconceived categories. That isn't to say that semantic categories must be entirely abandoned. In fact, I will circle back to the General Inquirer later in this chapter and use it casually to abbreviate description of a few patterns. But the word *casually*, in that last sentence, expresses a deliberate restraint. I have been careful throughout this book not to put much evidentiary weight on lists of words. While fixed semantic categories may be useful as loose abbreviations, we cannot trust them to describe cultural phenomena precisely. For trustworthy description, we need some kind of evidence more deeply rooted in historical context.

Modeling

Scholars who apply quantitative methods to literary history often turn up the kind of dramatic but puzzling pattern we encountered in the last section. Here the pattern took the form of a striking semantic trend that was difficult to interpret. But scholars often find themselves similarly squinting at networks of characters or authors, wondering what the shape of the network implies. The fundamental source of this problem is that researchers have begun by tracing phenomena that don't yet have literary significance for a community of readers. Although I know what colors are, for instance, I don't really know what the frequent occurrence of color terms in a novel would tell me about the story. "The chromatic novel" is not a genre anyone recognizes. An unfamiliar starting point can be fruitful, in the sense that it reveals large patterns scholars don't yet understand. But it doesn't help us interpret the patterns we discover. Revealing a new trend without connecting it to existing scholarly debate invites the question, "So what?" Researchers with a more quantitative background might characterize the problem as "data dredging": in sorting through a vast heap of evidence for something interesting, we run a risk of cherry-picking.

Both problems can be addressed in the same way: we need to reverse the sequence of steps in our inquiry. Instead of measuring things, finding patterns, and then finally asking what they mean, we need to start with an interpretive hypothesis (a "meaning" to investigate) and invent a way to test it.[20] The idea of starting with a hypothesis may hint at a parallel to a method of inquiry that has performed well since philosophers started using it in the seventeenth century. But in the twenty-first century, the word *science* has acquired a controversial prominence. For the moment, it may be less distracting to say that inquiry about the past needs to be guided by explicit theories. Open-ended exploration has value. But scholars lost in a vast digital library eventually need to constrain their flexibility by defining a specific question about concepts familiar to readers.

We happen to have encountered a question of that kind in figure 1.2, which seemed to suggest that our familiar concepts of fiction and biography diverged in the nineteenth century. I say that the illustration only "seemed to suggest" these genres were diverging, because they diverged in a vertical space we defined by arbitrarily choosing to count particular words. We could al-

20. The procedure I am suggesting reverses the order of steps suggested in Franco Moretti, "Patterns and Interpretation," Stanford Literary Lab Pamphlet 15, September 2017, https://litlab.stanford.edu/LiteraryLabPamphlet15.pdf.

most as easily define a list of words that would make the genres converge. So readers have no reason yet to conclude that novels became less like biographies in any general sense. In fact, there is some reason to suspect the opposite. Early-nineteenth-century novels are often Gothic and sensational; realists later in the century are said to have rejected the romance tradition in order to embrace description of the actual world in "common, ordinary language."[21] That shift sounds like something that might plausibly have *reduced* the stylistic distance between fiction and nonfiction.

But if the divergence of genres in figure 1.2 is puzzling and seems at odds with some existing accounts of literary history, why not take it as a hypothesis to test? That approach has the enormous advantage of beginning from a familiar starting point. Fiction and biography are not crisp, stable, or objective concepts; they are much less stable, in fact, than our concept of color. But unlike the "chromatic novel," fiction and biography are concepts that have long circulated through interpretive communities. To tell a meaningful story about the human past, we don't need stable objectivity. We need the foundation provided by recognizable social points of reference.[22]

But how would we test a hypothesis about the divergence or convergence of genres? There are many ways of measuring the stylistic distance between texts. Once again, we need to constrain this inquiry, in order to focus it. Instead of using any definition of similarity that seems plausible, we can use whatever method most reliably discriminates fiction from biography in a blind test. Since we cannot assume that the differences between genres will remain the same across the timeline, we'll need to use different tests for different periods. If the most accurate discriminator we can find for each period becomes more accurate as we move down the timeline, that will be fairly solid evidence that fiction

---

21. Ronald E. Martin, *American Literature and the Destruction of Knowledge: Innovative Writing in the Age of Epistemology* (Durham, NC: Duke University Press, 1991), 109.
22. Stanley Fish, "Interpreting the 'Variorum,'" *Critical Inquiry* 2, no. 3 (1976): 465–85.

and biography were separated by growing stylistic differences. In effect, we are reversing the process that created figure 1.2: instead of starting with a list of significant words and asking how two genres fare against that standard, we are starting from the genres, looking for textual differences that distinguish them, and then evaluating the strength of the differences.

Since we want to distinguish fiction from nonfiction using only evidence contained in the text, this task will probably need to be delegated to an algorithm. Human readers would find it hard to forget their previous knowledge that Samuel Johnson had a real existence and Robinson Crusoe only a feigned one. So this is where the technical innovations of the last forty years start to matter. Up to this point in the chapter, computers have been dispensable conveniences. With a few days of hard work, we could have counted words by hand. But now we need something more complex: a test that can distinguish volumes of fiction from biographies. This requires us to define a model—a relation between variables—instead of a single axis of measurement. On one side, we have the probability that librarians will label a given volume "fiction." Call this the predicted variable. On the other side, we have a host of predictors: whatever linguistic features turn out to signal genre. We need, in essence, a way of connecting those predictor variables to the predicted one with an equals sign. The result will be an equation that estimates the probability that a volume will be perceived as fiction—in other words, a *statistical model* of genre.

Statistical models are uncommon in the humanities, and humanists may initially suspect that such a model could only answer questions that fit our understanding of science. For instance, scientific categories are often imagined to lack ambiguity. Will a quantitative model be able to handle uncertainty? To use numbers, won't we have to posit a crisp boundary between fiction and biography?

That would certainly be an odd choice. Literary scholars know that the boundaries between genres are blurry. Memoirs can be fictionalized, novels can be *à clef.* Fortunately, statistical models are good at blurriness. In fact, the imprecision of the human world is part of the reason why numbers are so useful in social science: they allow researchers to describe continua instead of sorting everything into discrete categories. Our model of genre will similarly be continuous. We will have to train it on a sample of volumes that librarians have sorted into two discrete groups (fiction and biography) because the human beings who wander through libraries tend to prefer a space organized by clear boundaries. But the model itself doesn't have to be discrete; it predicts the *probability* that a volume will be perceived as fiction. We can use that probability to test the model in yes/no fashion, treating anything above 50% probability as a *yes*. But we can also use probabilities to place volumes on a continuum where nothing is purely fictional or nonfictional. If we wanted, we could make our definition of genre even more complex. For instance, in this experiment, volumes have been labeled mostly by late-twentieth-century librarians, although the volumes themselves range across three centuries. If reliance on contemporary observers troubled us, we could build a model where genre categories are subdivided to represent the perspectives of different observers—and we'll do exactly that in chapter 2.

What linguistic features should the model use as clues? The choice is not actually crucial. A researcher could draw up a list of hypothetical differences between fiction and biography and handcraft a list of features. Dialogue may be more common in fiction, for instance, so we could construct a special-purpose system that distinguished fiction from biography by counting lines of dialogue. But it would be a waste of effort, because the prominence of dialogue (along with many other details that predict genre) will be easier to capture on the level of word choice. Books with a lot of dialogue will tend to include tags like *said* and *exclaimed*, for instance, as well as interjections like *oh* and *yes*. So a flexible strategy, which has worked well for many similar questions, is simply to treat each dictionary entry (and type of punctuation) as a variable. If 1.2% of the words in a particular volume are *the*, the value of *the* for that volume will be 0.012. The model itself can become a set of coefficients assigned to dictionary entries. If words common in fiction are given larger coefficients, then multiplying the frequency of each word by its coefficient and adding up all the multiplied values will produce higher probabilities for volumes of fiction. The tricky part of this, clearly, is assigning the coefficients. That is done by a learning algorithm, which tries to assign coefficients that separate fiction from biography as accurately as possible in a training set of labeled volumes.

Readers unfamiliar with this method are often disconcerted by the seeming naïveté of representing literary works simply through word frequency. It would be easy to add complexity to soothe skeptics. Ad hoc syntactic variables might make the model seem more likely to capture the loosely defined concept we gesture at with the word *style*. But candidly, this would be no more than a magician's puff of smoke, which impresses viewers by distracting them from the actual mechanics of the trick. In reality, models based on word frequency predict human readers' judgments as well as more complex strategies.[23] This doesn't mean that the differences between texts are, at bottom, all differences of diction. The fundamental difference between biography and fiction probably has something to do with our concept of reality (hard as that may be to define). But a learning algorithm doesn't attempt to define the fundamental difference between two genres; it aims simply to distinguish examples. And in practice, the thematic and formal differences between genres do leave legible traces at the level of word choice. Deferring definition is a philosophically interesting aspect of machine learning, discussed at more length in appendix B. For now, suffice it to say that literary historians may appreciate the flexibility of this approach, since literary genres rarely have clear and stable definitions.

There are many learning algorithms; the one I use throughout this book is logistic regression, used for many decades in

23. Alessandro Moschitti and Roberto Basili, "Complex Linguistic Features for Text Classification: A Comprehensive Study," *Proceedings of the 26th European Conference on Information Retrieval* (2004): 181–96. For reflections on the concept of meaning that emerges from attending to the mere frequency of words, see Piper, *Enumerations*, 13–20.

the social sciences. The only thing modern about this method is that I add "regularization"—a degree of deliberate blurriness that prevents the model from memorizing the examples in its training set, forcing it instead to produce a looser, more portable generalization. We can test whether a model is truly portable by asking how well it performs on a test set—a group of volumes held out from training so the model can make blind predictions. By repeating the test with different groups of held-out volumes, we can cover the whole corpus; this is called cross-validation, and it produces an estimate of the model's real accuracy on previously unseen examples.

If we apply this strategy to the same volumes graphed in figure 1.2, we find that the boundary between fiction and biography is relatively easy to model. An initial tuning step reveals that models tend to be most accurate when they include the eleven hundred words most common in the corpus. When we train models of that size across the three-century timeline, we get accuracies ranging from 87% to 100%. To reveal how much of that variation is random, I have trained fifteen models in each twenty-year period, using a different random sample of 150 volumes each time. Figure 1.3 plots the accuracy of each model as a diamond. The curve is by no means smooth, but in general this picture suggests that the divergence of genres in figure 1.2 was a broad trend, not limited to the question of "concrete diction." It is relatively hard to distinguish fiction from biography in the eighteenth century (accuracy is below 95%), and it seems to get easier to tell these genres apart as we move forward—at least up to the twentieth century.

But "accuracy" is a crude metric, which reduces a probabilistic model to a binary choice. Moreover, since all of these models are fairly accurate, figure 1.3 really only informs us about extreme cases that are unusually hard to recognize. In figure 1.4, we take better advantage of the model's flexibility by using the vertical axis to report the exact probabilities the model assigned to different volumes. Gray circles were biography according to librarians, and black triangles were fiction. I have run a separate model

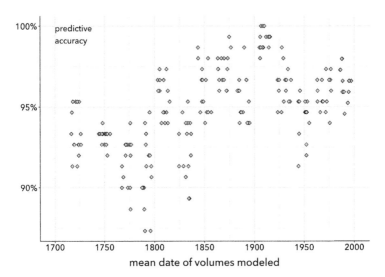

FIGURE I.3. Predictive accuracy of models that attempt to distinguish fiction from biography.

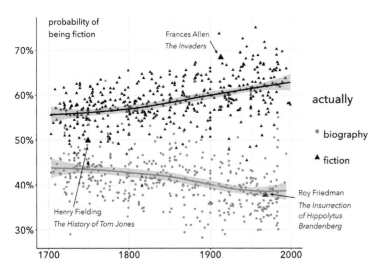

FIGURE I.4. Probability of being fiction or biography. Statistical models of genre make predictions about 890 volumes of fiction and biography evenly distributed from 1700 to 1999.

for each half century, so volumes aren't judged by anachronistic standards, but a roughly similar pattern appears if we model the whole set at once. One can see that the models tend to become more confident in their judgment as time passes. Early volumes are often fairly ambiguous, hovering close to the central dividing line. (*Tom Jones*, in fact, is exactly on the line.) But twentieth-century books tend to be more clearly marked as either fiction or biography.

A statistical model's inference about probability is admittedly an odd thing to discuss. It is much less tangible than "the frequency of color terms," where we began. In fact, I feel confident that this book will be criticized for talking about models: many readers would find distant reading more accessible if it confined itself to linguistic measurements like sentence length or word frequency. Instead of directly measuring the text, predictive models describe a relationship between social and textual evidence. This inevitably requires some mental gymnastics, but in the long run I think this relational approach grounds interpretation more persuasively in human history. Figure 1.1, measuring the frequency of color terms, was simple and vivid—but it was hard to say exactly what it meant. By contrast, figures 1.3 and 1.4 have clear historical significance, because we started by looking for a difference between two genres that human readers already recognize. Moreover, this strategy will provide an important kind of perspectival flexibility in later chapters. This chapter has taken the difference between fiction and biography as a constant. (I have trusted librarians to define the genres.) But if we chose, we could train different models to capture different readers' understanding of this generic boundary. When we discuss boundaries even slipperier than fiction/nonfiction, that flexibility will become indispensable.

The words that matter in figures 1.3 and 1.4 are, simply, whatever words worked best to distinguish fiction from biography in a given period; they were chosen by a regression algorithm that was struggling to separate these two groups of texts. We found that the best available separation tended to be clearer in the nineteenth century than in the eighteenth and clearer in the

TABLE 1.1. Categories that distinguish fiction from biography. The frequency of 118 semantic categories from the Harvard General Inquirer was calculated for the 890 volumes plotted in figure 1.4. Then the categories were sorted by correlation with the volumes' predicted probabilities of being fiction.

Correlate with fiction	r	Correlate with biography	r
Action verbs	.815	Political terms	.741
Body parts	.723	Organized systems of belief	.730
Verbs of sensory perception	.720	Abstract means	.726
Verbs of dialogue	.684	Power	.692
Physical adjectives	.683	Economic terms	.675

twentieth century than in the nineteenth. In the later twentieth century, the binary accuracy in figure 1.3 moves differently than the mean probability in figure 1.4—which is to say, there may be more radical outliers after 1930: things like *The Insurrection of Hippolytus Brandenberg* (1969), an odd Pynchonesque epistolary novel that looks a lot like a biography.[24] But the median twentieth-century volume is still easier to recognize than it was in the nineteenth century.

Moreover, if we look at the words that actually distinguish works of fiction from biography and sort them into categories borrowed from the General Inquirer, we see above all—our old friends—descriptive action verbs, body parts, verbs of physical perception like "see" and "hear," and physical adjectives (table 1.1). At this point an incandescent light bulb should appear somewhere over these pages because we are getting close to understanding a question we have pursued throughout the chapter. Heuser and Le-Khac originally noticed that concrete words became steadily more common in nineteenth-century fiction; their research had nothing to do with nonfiction. I pointed out that the words they identified don't rise in biographies, merely to note an odd fact that would complicate a broad social explanation for rising concreteness, such as urbanization. But now we see that the gap between fiction and biography was no accident. When

24. Roy Friedman, *The Insurrection of Hippolytus Brandenberg* (New York: Macmillan, 1969).

we try to model the differences between fiction and biography, we rediscover exactly the words whose rise Heuser and Le-Khac were trying to explain. To put this another way: the direction fiction moved from 1750 to 1950 can be concisely described as "away from biography." It begins to look like the novel steadily specialized in something that biography (and other forms of nonfiction) could rarely provide: descriptions of bodies, physical actions, and immediate sensory perceptions in a precisely specified place and time.

Table 1.1 lists the semantic categories from the Harvard General Inquirer that correlate most strongly with the model's predictions that a work is fiction or biography. The Pearson correlation coefficient, r, measures the strength of a linear relationship between two variables, relative to other variation in the data. By loose scientific convention, absolute values of r around .1 are called small effects; those around .3 are medium-sized effects; those greater than .5 are large effects.[25] The correlations in table 1.1 are all rather large effects.

Of course, using the General Inquirer also brings us back to semantic categories, and I have already stressed that lists of words are an imperfect anchor for interpretation. Lists of "body parts" may not change very much, but what does the General Inquirer mean by "power," for instance? How can we trust that these semantic categories (developed mostly by psychologists in the 1960s) will remain appropriate for our whole timeline?

My answer is simply that we shouldn't. The General Inquirer has no special authority, and I have tried not to make its quirks a load-bearing element of this argument. The Inquirer's specific definition of "power" will not be important here; all I need to take from table 1.1 is a broad contrast between immediate sensory perception and social collectivity. We could reach that conclusion in many other ways. Andrew Piper's study "Fictionality" uses a different set of semantic categories but ends in the same place: modern fiction is distinguished from nonfiction by emphasiz-

---

25. Jacob Cohen, "A Power Primer," *Psychological Bulletin* 112, no. 1 (1992): 155–59.

ing "sensorial input and embodied entities."[26] Or we could use semantic categories developed at Stanford. These are based on nineteenth-century discursive patterns instead of twentieth-century social science, but they produce the same result: fiction differs from biography by emphasizing concrete description instead of social generalization.

In short, historical interpreters often have to accept that there is no single authoritative account of the past. This can be frustrating—especially when numbers are involved, since we associate numbers with objectivity. But instead of seeking an objective metric to solve the problem, the best course of action is often to consider different perspectives. Sometimes the perspectives will importantly diverge; in that case it becomes necessary to particularize the differences between them (as we'll do in chapter 2). But often different perspectives largely agree, and the historical interpreter can summarize their general drift with an illustrative example.[27] Table 1.1 is an illustrative example of that kind. I trust it not because the General Inquirer is authoritative but because I have looked at this evidence from many other angles.

For instance, when I wrote above that fiction gradually specializes in portraying "immediate sensory perceptions in a precisely specified place and time," I was not relying purely on lists of words. I mentioned precisely specified times because I also happen to know that fiction moved toward description of ever-briefer scenes in this same period. To measure the pace of narration, two colleagues and I read about sixteen hundred passages, of 250 words each, from biography and fiction published in the last three centuries.[28] Estimating the length of time described in each

26. Andrew Piper, "Fictionality," *Cultural Analytics*, December 2016, http://culturalanalytics.org/2016/12/fictionality/.
27. For the value of acknowledging the researcher's own involvement in interpretation, see Andrew Gelman and Christian Hennig, "Beyond Subjective and Objective in Statistics," *Journal of the Royal Statistical Society: Series A (Statistics in Society)* 180, no. 4 (2017): 967–1033.
28. Ted Underwood, "Why Literary Time Is Measured in Minutes," *ELH* 85, no. 2 (2018): 341–65. Data for the article were gathered in collaboration with Sabrina Lee and Jessica Mercado.

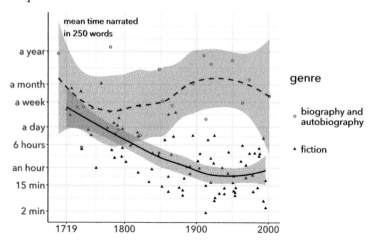

FIGURE 1.5. Mean time narrated in 250 words, 1700–2000. Biographies continue to describe life at the scale of a week or a month, while novels move toward a more finely divided scale of temporal description.

passage can admittedly be tricky: narrated time is by no means linear. But in practice, readers largely agreed with each other: pairs of estimates about passages correlated at $r = .78$. Looking at the history of narrative pace across three hundred years (figure 1.5), we found a pattern that roughly tracks the differentiation shown in figures 1.2–1.4: the pace of biographies remained relatively steady, while the pace of fiction dramatically slowed. In the eighteenth century it is common for several days to pass on each page of a novel. But by the twentieth century, the average 250-word passage of fiction describes a period of only thirty minutes. Moreover, the novels with the slowest pace also tended to use the most concrete diction. So we have reason to suspect that changes in pacing and in descriptive vocabulary happened not only at the same time but for interlocking reasons.

There are some wrinkles here that will require decades to iron out. I have been describing trends, not motives or market forces. So I can't prove that novelists moved toward sensory and temporal immediacy *because* it was a niche not yet filled by nonfiction. When I say that fiction and nonfiction "differentiated" from each other, I am loosely guided by Émile Durkheim's theory that social institutions tend to subdivide and specialize.[29] But his theory doesn't provide a detailed account of causes or motives. The motives of writers and readers, across three centuries, will no doubt be varied and tangled.

Later chapters of this book will take a few steps toward untangling social forces, but they remain cautious about causal explanation. Nor is explanation necessarily the most important goal of a study like this one. Causal questions become a bit tautological on a scale of centuries, since the loop from cause to effect to cause again may have cycled through hundreds of times. For trends on this scale, rich description is often more illuminating. And this chapter has already described a striking trend: the narrative pace and thematic emphases of fiction have become steadily less like nonfiction for three hundred years. In chapter 3, moreover, we will discover that stylistic changes in poetry parallel the changes we have seen in fiction. So the little clue of color vocabulary in *The Invaders* has now led us to a trend that can be described generally as the emergence of a widening gulf between literary and nonliterary language. Subsequent chapters will unfold that trend in more detail, showing how the literariness of poems and stories was increasingly defined as temporal immediacy and concreteness.

Coordinating Different Scales of Analysis

A chapter that covers as much ground as this one will leave many questions unanswered. The broad trend I have characterized as a differentiation of fiction from biography could be broken into overlapping pieces—changes in point of view, pacing, or subject matter, taking place across different stretches of the timeline. A full exploration of the phenomenon might separate all those things and explain how they are related. But the title of this chapter is not "Now, at last, we fully understand the outlines of

29. Émile Durkheim, *The Division of Labor in Society* (New York: Free Press, 1964).

literary history." I began by posing a question about our perception that the literary past had been broadly mapped, exactly to make that illusion of comprehension disappear. Leaving loose ends was always the point of the exercise.

On the other hand, a magician's task isn't finished, a recent screenplay has reminded us, after making "something disappear." You also "have to bring it back. That's why every magic trick has a third act, the hardest part, the part we call 'The Prestige.'"[30] This chapter may not answer every question it raised, but it ought to try to bring back some of the comprehension that vanished as we zoomed out to an unfamiliar scale. In shifting from simple measurement to models of genre, I was already struggling to restore comprehension, by reattaching large, cloudy lexical trends to recognizable literary reference points. Another way to bring back comprehension is to acknowledge that, in a sense, we did already understand every individual segment of the trend we are discussing.

For instance, it has long been understood that the early-eighteenth-century novel developed its peculiar form of realism by echoing biography and autobiography. Robinson Crusoe keeps a diary; Pamela Andrews writes letters in every spare moment; Henry Fielding outright calls himself a "biographer" in *The History of Tom Jones*. Ian Watt influentially argued that the novel only achieved maturity when Jane Austen set this charade aside, inventing a way to sustain "Defoe's and Richardson's psychological closeness to the subjective world of the characters" without the "trickery" of feigned autobiography.[31] So the widening distance between fictional and nonfictional lives in the eighteenth century is very much what we might expect to see there.

The history of nineteenth-century fiction has not usually been understood as a continued differentiation from biographical form. But theories of nineteenth-century realism are indirectly

30. Jonathan Nolan and Christopher Nolan, screenplay for *The Prestige*, based on *The Prestige*, by Christopher Priest (London: Faber and Faber, 2006).

31. Fielding, *Tom Jones*, 414; Watt, *Rise of the Novel*, 297.

compatible with many of the stylistic changes we have traced in this chapter. For instance, Peter Brooks has argued that "realism more than almost any other mode of literature makes sight paramount," an observation that Nancy Armstrong and Michael McKeon have explained by connecting the realist novel to new visual technologies like photography.[32] These scholars would hardly be shocked to discover that physical adjectives and verbs of sensory perception (notably "see") are rising in nineteenth-century fiction. Coming from a converse perspective on realism, Georg Lukács would shake his head sadly looking at table 1.1, not at all surprised that evasion of direct reference to politics and economics is one of the trends that increasingly distinguishes the novel from nonfiction.[33]

Finally, our preliminary discussion of *The Invaders* has already shown us that scholars of modernism could also find much to recognize in the novel's growing distance from biography. The decline of omniscient narration in the early twentieth century is usually painted as a rejection of Victorian novelists' garrulous dear-readerism. But it could just as easily be understood as bidding farewell to a basic premise of nonfiction. To locate the point of view in characters with limited knowledge of the story creates a final and decisive formal separation between fiction and nonfiction narrative.

In short, scholars already have some explanation for every part of the widening gap between fiction and biography. It would be odd if they didn't. Thousands of human beings have spent a great deal of time studying literary history, and we understand that history, locally, very well. But local understanding doesn't necessarily tell us how all the pieces fit together to form a big picture. The juxtaposition of local knowledge with global ignorance

32. Brooks, *Realist Vision*, 3; Nancy Armstrong, *Fiction in the Age of Photography: The Legacy of British Realism* (Cambridge, MA: Harvard University Press, 1999); Michael McKeon, "Photography, Film, and the Novel," in *Theory of the Novel: A Historical Approach*, ed. McKeon (Baltimore: Johns Hopkins University Press, 2000), 657–58.

33. Georg Lukács, *The Historical Novel*, trans. Hannah and Stanley Mitchell (Boston: Beacon, 1962).

can be irritating, and our minds move rapidly to erase any dissonance between the two. When large patterns finally emerge, they are necessarily compatible with pieces of the puzzle we have already seen at close range. So an observer inevitably feels "I recognize that! I knew *Tom Jones* was akin to biography!" From there, it is a short step to the conclusion that the global pattern was also lurking at the back of my mind or was nothing more than I expected all along. But this is often self-deception. Psychologists call it "hindsight bias." I started by contrasting Henry Fielding to Frances Allen partly in order to remind readers how literary scholars have usually framed arguments about long timelines in the past. Typically, these arguments have been vague, controversial assertions: for instance, fans of modernism will advance a thesis about a shift from telling to showing, which immediately annoys fans of the Victorian novel. The challenge is to find a perspective that makes the descriptions preferred by eighteenth-, nineteenth-, and twentieth-century scholars all congruent with each other.

The temptation to see macroscopic discoveries as less than genuinely new is particularly strong for literary scholars because we are trained to find disciplinary significance only in claims that directly reverse existing expectations. When we are writing about individual books, this is a reasonable goal. A single book is easy to summarize. So if I plan to write about a novel you already read, I need to directly reverse some of your expectations in order to tell you anything new. But when we are surveying three centuries of literary history, descriptive summary is barely possible. Privileging counterintuitive claims here would be as absurd as privileging counterintuitive arguments about climate change. The truth is that we barely have intuitions about patterns on this scale; our expectations are not clearly formed yet, and it would be just as important to confirm them as to confute them.

The expectations we do articulate clearly are often stories about contrast and conflict. So realistic novels are said to critique the romance tradition, modernists supposedly reject Victorian omniscience, and postmodernists react against modernist hostility to mass culture.[34] Scholars know this narrative of conflict and displacement is a rhetorical crutch, and we frequently apologize for it when sharing a drink with colleagues who work on earlier periods. But we also keep making the gesture because we don't have many better ways to link a long series of roughly generation-sized studies and turn them into a connected narrative.

Quantitative methods give scholars a different way of connecting the dots—one that makes it easier to reveal gradual change across a long timeline. But this large picture doesn't necessarily erase more familiar stories about generational struggle and dialectical reversal. Those conflicts merely occupy a different scale of description. Literary history can be a series of fierce battles between different aesthetic standards and also a single smooth current carrying the novel steadily away from the language, subject matter, and formal strategies of nonfiction narrative. If we approach to examine that historical current more closely, the things that looked like eddies will turn out to be struggles between aesthetic movements.[35] Approaching even closer, we may see individual authors floating on the surface—for instance, here is one who lost her hearing and worked as a photographer. And here are two young people, facing each other in a small boat, surrounded by sun-flecked water. The wind has caught her hair and the ends of her black four-in-hand tie.

34. Perry Miller, "The Romance and the Novel," in *Nature's Nation* (Cambridge, MA: Harvard University Press, 1967), 241–78; Andreas Huyssen, *After the Great Divide: Modernism, Mass Culture, Postmodernism* (Bloomington: Indiana University Press, 1987).

35. Throughout this book, my emphasis on a *longue durée* is indebted to the Annales school. As Alan Liu has rightly observed, my watery metaphor here precisely reproduces Fernand Braudel's contrast between the slow rhythms of social and environmental history and "the history of events: surface disturbances, crests of foam that the tides of history carry on their strong backs." Fernand Braudel, *The Mediterranean and the Mediterranean World in the Age of Philip II*, 2nd rev. ed., trans. Siân Reynolds (Berkeley: University of California Press, 1995), 1:21.

2

The Life Spans of Genres

Although debates about genre are as old as literary criticism itself, the term is still only loosely defined. Part of the reason is that genres look like different things at different points in the life of a text. Scholars of rhetoric, interested in the creation of works, tend to interpret genres as communicative actions.[1] Sociologists often emphasize communities of readers.[2] Literary scholars, for their part, are preoccupied with the patterning of the texts themselves. Of course, all of these aspects of genre are connected. But it doesn't follow that the histories of production, reception, and form are precisely the same. Does the persistence of science fiction fandom, for instance, imply that a single textual pattern has united works of science fiction themselves, from the pulp era to the present? Many scholars are skeptical. Some argue that "there is no such *thing* as science fiction" in the texts themselves: the history of a genre is only the history of a community of readers, who may use the term "science fiction" to describe radically different things in different decades.[3]

1. Carolyn Miller, "Genre as Social Action," *Quarterly Journal of Speech* 70 (1984): 151–67.
2. Pierre Bourdieu, *Distinction: A Social Critique of the Judgment of Taste* (Cambridge, MA: Harvard University Press, 1984); Paul DiMaggio, "Classification in Art," *American Sociological Review* 52 (1987): 440–55.
3. Mark Bould and Sherryl Vint, "There is No Such Thing as Science Fiction," in *Reading Science Fiction*, ed. James Gunn, Marleen Barr, and Matthew Candelaria (New York: Palgrave, 2009), 43.

Science fiction is not the only genre raising problems of this kind. Some scholars trace contemporary detective fiction, for instance, to a durable model established by Edgar Allan Poe in the 1840s. But Franco Moretti has suggested that genres rarely survive longer than a single generation. In that case, the superficial continuity of the term "detective fiction" might cover a series of different forms (the Holmesian "case," the closed circle of country-house suspects, the crime thriller), linked by inheritance more than direct similarity. Maurizio Ascari pushes this theory of flux even farther, arguing that "all genres change ceaselessly," and crime fiction no longer has much to do with Poe at all.[4]

These questions about the life spans of genres remain perplexing because they are deeply perspectival. Our disagreement is not fundamentally about texts or about the history of reception but about the possibility of comparing different historical vantage points. Everyone admits, for instance, that scientific romances by Mary Shelley and Jules Verne differ substantially from the twentieth-century phenomenon that Hugo Gernsback named "science fiction." But everyone also admits that contemporary readers of science fiction often perceive nineteenth-century romances as examples of the genre they enjoy. The controversial question is whether these perceived continuities are simply retrospective projections. It remains a difficult question because history only moves in one direction. We have no way to avoid thinking of science fiction when we read Jules Verne, so it is hard to know whether to trust our perception of continuity. Readers in 1865, conversely, had no opportunity to think of *science fiction*, since the phrase didn't yet exist. We might like to travel back to 1865, offer readers our concept of science fiction, and ask how well it describes Verne's position in their own world. But of course, if we had a time machine, we wouldn't need to define science fiction at all.

---

4. Franco Moretti, *Graphs, Maps, Trees: Abstract Models for Literary History* (New York: Verso, 2005), 18–22; Maurizio Ascari, "The Dangers of Distant Reading: Reassessing Moretti's Approach to Literary Genres," *Genre* 47, no. 1 (2014): 15.

In this chapter, predictive models will become not quite a time machine but something almost as useful: a memory-wiping flashbulb that allows us to strategically erase our knowledge of the future or past as needed. The computer knows nothing about literary history: it models only the evidence we give it. This useful blindness will allow us to provisionally bracket twentieth-century science fiction and to model Verne purely by contrasting him to his nineteenth-century contemporaries. Then we can compare those models to models of the twentieth-century genre and see how closely their predictions align. In the pages that follow, I will call this method "perspectival modeling." This chapter will often literally be modeling the perspectives of different groups of readers, but the phrase could also apply more broadly to any strategy that gets leverage on cultural history by comparing models trained on different subsets of the evidence. The end of this chapter will assess the pace of change, for instance, by comparing models trained on different periods.[5]

The strength of this method comes from something that might appear to be its weakness. A supervised model learns only from the examples we give it. This means that its predictions have a purely relative significance. The model cannot measure any universal dimension of language; it just indicates whether a given text more closely resembles the examples in group A or group B. At first, the relative character of this evidence may appear to undermine the whole point of quantification. We often imagine numbers as an objective yardstick—something like sentence length or linguistic entropy that can become a fixed reference point for the flux of history. A supervised model, by contrast, provides only a circular sort of evidence: it describes one set of texts through their relation to another.

But then, circularity has long been recognized as the inherent condition of historical interpretation.[6] Events and artifacts ac-

5. The germ of insight for this method came from Michael Witmore, "The Time Problem: Rigid Classifiers, Classifier Postmarks," *Wine Dark Sea*, April 16, 2012, http:// winedarksea.org/?p=1507.

6. Wilhelm Dilthey, *The Formation of the Historical World in the Human Sciences* (1910; Princeton, NJ: Princeton University Press, 2002), 280–81.

quire meaning only in relation to other parts of history: they are always interpreted in relation to their own historical context, as well as other contexts implicitly brought to bear by an interpreter. So a method that provides relative and contextual description may be exactly what we need to orient ourselves in this space. When researchers try to step outside history to find a fixed metric like sentence length, they often end up creating a measurement whose significance is hard to define. Human significance is created only by human history. For that reason, perspectival modeling will become this book's central source of leverage on the past—both in this chapter's arguments about genre and in subsequent arguments about gender and literary prestige.

This mode of analysis is admittedly more complex than simply measuring linguistic features of the text. But it becomes complex in order to address a problem fundamental to the humanities. Statistical models can embrace the contextual and perspectival character of historical interpretation, while giving scholars more control over the contexts and perspectives they provisionally adopt. This will never allow us to entirely escape our own historical situation. Although the models in this chapter rely on books labeled by many different hands across hundreds of years, they are still produced in the twenty-first century, with twenty-first-century methods. (As I have said, a model is not literally a time machine.) But perspectival modeling does at least allow us to represent the perspectives of other eras, in a form solid enough to allow one perspective to be compared rigorously to another.

The models of genre created in this chapter will rely on textual evidence. But that doesn't force us to assume that genres are fundamentally textual patterns. As I began by noting, genres wear several different faces: they are practices of literary production, horizons of readerly expectation, and textual templates, all at once. If I had to choose one of those three faces as primary, I would lean toward emphasizing readers' expectations. So this chapter will initially define a "genre" as a group of books recognized by some specific, historically situated group of readers—whether they are nineteenth-century reviewers arguing about sensation novels or twentieth-century librarians shelving books under "Detective Fiction." Textual similarity will enter this chapter's argument only because it turns out that texts can in fact be used to predict readers' responses. A model trained on a sample of texts that reviewers labeled "detective fiction" can identify other books that the same reviewers labeled the same way.[7] In other words, text will function here as a medium, registering definitions of genre that are in themselves fundamentally social. One advantage of the textual medium is that it allows us to compare definitions formed in different historical contexts and expressed through groups of illustrative examples that may not overlap.

What Story Should We Expect to Find?

Since literary scholars adhere to radically different theories of genre, we might expect several different outcomes for this inquiry. If Mark Bould and Sherryl Vint are right that "there is no such *thing*" as genre in the text itself—only a contested set of expectations defined and redefined by marketing—then we might expect textual models of genre simply to fail. If Franco Moretti is right that genre is a generational phenomenon, we might expect textual models to be stable only for twenty or thirty years. Science fiction, in particular, seems likely to be mutable, since submarines and ray guns are constantly replaced by new wonders of tomorrow. It is not self-evident that the textual patterns in science fiction would persist for more than a few decades.

On the other hand, we might just as reasonably expect to find a different pattern. With genre-specific pulp magazines (like *Amazing Stories*) and imprints (like Harlequin), twentieth-century genres achieved an institutional solidity that had rarely

---

7. This chapter's work on genre was inspired by several trailblazing experiments. Brett Kessler, Geoffrey Nunberg, and Hinrich Schütze, "Automatic Detection of Text Genre," *Proceedings of the Eighth Conference of the European Chapter of the Association for Computational Linguistics* (1997): 32–38; Sarah Allison, Ryan Heuser, Matthew Jockers, Franco Moretti, and Michael Witmore, "Quantitative Formalism: An Experiment," Stanford Literary Lab Pamphlet 1, January 15, 2011, https://litlab.stanford.edu/LiteraryLabPamphlet1.pdf; Matthew L. Jockers, *Macroanalysis: Digital Methods and Literary History* (Urbana: University of Illinois Press, 2013), 67–92.

been seen before. Histories of genre often emphasize the gradual consolidation of genre conventions in the first half of the twentieth century. Scholars of the detective story point to Ronald Knox's so-called Decalogue (1929) of rules for writers as a crystallizing moment.[8] For other genres the process of consolidation is thought to have taken even longer. Gary K. Wolfe suggests that "the science fiction novel persistently failed to cohere as a genre" until Pocket Books gave it institutional form in the 1940s.[9] If this account of literary history is correct, we might expect to find not a succession of generational phases but a steady hardening of boundaries, producing genres that are much more clearly distinct by the middle of the twentieth century than at its outset. Frankly, this is what I expected to find when I began the project.

To investigate these questions, I have gathered lists of titles assigned to a genre in eighteen different sites of reception.[10] Some of these lists reflect recent scholarly opinion; some were shaped by nineteenth-century reviewers; others reflect the practices of many different library catalogers over a long period of time. Although each list defines its object slightly differently, they can be loosely arranged around three master categories whose coherence I propose to test: detective fiction (or "mystery" or "crime" or "Newgate" fiction), science fiction (also defined in a variety of ways), and the Gothic. (It is debatable whether the Gothic, writ large, is a genre at all—but that's what makes it an interesting case.) I also collected texts corresponding to these titles, relying on the Chicago Text Lab and HathiTrust Digital Library as sources. By comparing groups of texts associated with different communities of reception and segments of the timeline, we can ask exactly how stable different categories have been.

8. Ronald Knox, introduction to *The Best Detective Stories of 1928–29*, ed. Ronald Knox, rpt. in *Murder for Pleasure: The Life and Times of the Detective Story*, ed. Howard Haycraft (New York: Biblio and Tannen, 1976), 251.

9. Gary K. Wolfe, *Evaporating Genres: Essays on Fantastic Literature* (Middletown, CT: Wesleyan University Press, 2011), 21.

10. For full metadata, see an online repository: Ted Underwood, "Data and Code to Support *Distant Horizons*," Zenodo, last modified March 25, 2018, http://doi.org/10.5281/zenodo.1206317.

The story that actually emerged from this experiment didn't line up very neatly with either of the patterns we might have expected to find: generational succession or gradual consolidation. I see little evidence of the generational waves that Moretti's theory would predict. In fact, it isn't even true that books in a chronologically focused genre (like "the sensation novel, 1860–1880") necessarily resemble each other more closely than books spread out across a long timeline. Detective fiction and science fiction display a textual coherence that is at least as strong as the shorter-lived genres Moretti discusses, and they sustain it over very long periods (160 or perhaps even 200 years). So I think we can set aside the conjecture that twenty-five-year generational cycles have special importance for the study of genre.

But I also haven't found much evidence for the story of gradual consolidation that I expected to find. Although it is clearly true that the publishing institutions governing genre developed gradually, it appears I was wrong to expect that the textual differences between genres would develop in the same gradual way. In the case of detective fiction, for instance, the textual differences that distinguish twentieth-century stories of detection from other genres can be traced back very clearly as far as "The Murders in the Rue Morgue"—and not much farther. Detective fiction did spread gradually, in the sense that Poe and Eugène Vidocq were initially isolated figures, without a supporting cast of imitators, let alone genre-specific magazines and book clubs. But textual patterns don't have to develop as gradually as institutions do. Poe's stories already display many of the same features that distinguish twentieth-century crime fiction from other genres. Science fiction turns out to be almost equally stable, over an equally long span of time—which is a bit surprising, because the dominant critical story about science fiction strongly implies that it failed to consolidate until the twentieth century. These findings push in the opposite direction from much contemporary scholarship. Instead of being more volatile than communities of reception, textual patterns turn out to be, if anything, more durable.

Predictive Modeling

Computers enter this chapter largely to address a tangle of problems created by recent genre theory. If we could define genres once and for all by locating a single formal principle that unified them, the critic's task would be much simpler. We could say that science fiction is Darko Suvin's "literature of cognitive estrangement," and be done.[11] Unfortunately, readers rarely agree about the defining characteristic of a genre; different communities may choose to emphasize different features of the same works. Genre theorists increasingly suspect that genres are "family resemblances," constituted by a host of overlapping features.[12] Moreover, genres are historical constructions: the features that matter may change.[13]

In short, it increasingly seems that a genre is not a single object we can observe and describe. It may instead be a mutable set of relations between works that are linked in different ways and resemble each other to different degrees. A problem like this requires a methodology that is cautious about ontological assumptions and patient with details.

Predictive modeling fits the bill. Leo Breiman has emphasized that predictive models depart from familiar statistical methods (and I would add, from traditional critical procedures) by bracketing the quest to identify underlying factors that really cause and explain the phenomenon being studied.[14] Where genre is concerned, this means that our goal is no longer to intuit a definition but to find a model that can reproduce the judgments made by particular historical observers. For instance, adjectives of size ("huge," "gigantic," but also "tiny") are among the most reliable textual clues that a book will be called science fiction. Few crit-

11. Darko Suvin, "On the Poetics of the Science Fiction Genre," *College English* 34, no. 3 (1972): 372.

12. Paul Kincaid, "On the Origins of Genre," *Extrapolation* 44, no. 4 (2003): 413–14.

13. John Rieder, "On Defining SF," 193.

14. Breiman, "Statistical Modeling."

ics would define science fiction as a meditation on size, but it turns out that the works librarians categorize as science fiction do spend a lot of time talking about the topic. Add clues from a few hundred more words, and you may have a statistical model that can identify other works librarians called "science fiction," even if the underlying definition of the genre remains difficult to articulate (or never existed).

Hoyt Long and Richard Jean So have used predictive models in a similar way to recognize "latent, nonexplicit traces" of a haiku style in English poetry.[15] The point of machine learning in projects like these is not primarily to enlarge the number of books we consider but to register and compare blurry family resemblances that might be difficult to define verbally without reductiveness. We can dispense with fixed definitions and base the study of genre only on the practices of historically situated actors—but still produce models of genre substantive enough to compare and contrast. Here, and in many similar cases, computation can help scholars acknowledge the complexity of culture without collapsing the conversation into an empty consensus that all cultural phenomena are more or less slippery and elusive. Which genres turn out to be especially mutable or relatively stable?

Since no causal power is ascribed to variables in a predictive model, the particular features we use to model genres are not all-important. The models in this chapter will take the frequencies of words and marks of punctuation as clues, along with a few other simple measurements (average word length, for instance). But we could use other features of the text if we preferred. The choice of features turns out to make less difference than readers encountering text classification for the first time tend to assume, because genre is expressed redundantly on many different levels. Critical debates about genre, for instance, may emphasize structural aspects of plot. But open a novel to a random page, and read

---

15. Hoyt Long and Richard Jean So, "Literary Pattern Recognition: Modernism between Close Reading and Machine Learning," *Critical Inquiry* 42, no. 2 (2016): 266. For an earlier methodological model, see Jockers, *Macroanalysis*, 63–104.

a few paragraphs: without knowing the plot, you will quickly know whether you have opened a space opera or a detective story. Statistical models work by recognizing similar clues. Generally, efforts to improve genre classification by adding complexity to the model have turned out to be redundant: multiword phrases and information about character don't significantly improve on the accuracy of simple lexical models.[16]

Moreover, if all the models in this chapter could be improved by 1%, it would make no difference to the argument. What matter are the *relative* strengths of the boundaries between different groups of texts. Which generic groupings are easier or harder to detect? Making our models as accurate as possible is worth doing only because it's a reassuring sign that we haven't left evidence on the table that would have changed those rankings. Of course, confidence of this kind can only be provisional. The methods I use to train models in this chapter (and throughout the book) are commonly used for text classification: regularized logistic regression on several thousand features, mostly the frequencies of words in the texts (see appendix B for details). I cannot prove that no better methods will ever exist. All I can say is that lexical models capture human judgments about genre rather well (accuracy above 90% is not uncommon), and researchers have been trying for decades to find a better strategy, without much success. As I explain in appendix B, I tried many different variations myself before settling on this strategy.

It is still conceivable that these models could have blind spots. For instance, we might expect lexical models to perform poorly with science fiction across a long timeline, since the specific innovations that count as science fictional have a limited life span. If we found many cases of this type, we would have to question the value of modeling genre with lexical evidence. But in fact, we find something close to the reverse. Human readers may disagree

16. Lena Hettinger, Martin Becker, Isabella Riger, Fotis Jannidis, and Andreas Hotho, "Genre Classification on German Novels," 26th International Workshop on Database and Expert Systems Applications, 2015, http://www.uni-weimar.de/medien/webis/events/tir-15/tir15-papers-final/Hettinger2015-tir-paper.pdf.

about the continuity of Gernsback's "science fiction" with Verne's "scientific romance." But a lexical model has no difficulty grasping their similarity and is able to recognize science fiction across a long timeline with an accuracy of 90% or greater.

The challenges we encounter in modeling genre will usually come from excessive sensitivity, not from the coarseness we might expect to find in a quantitative model. The problem is not that lexical models fail to grasp the elusive similarities that define genres but that they turn out to be only too good at reproducing any category defined by human readers. Uncovering points of disagreement between readers will thus require a bit of ingenuity. For instance, if we fold the conflicting judgments of many readers together, an algorithm can usually still learn to recognize their areas of overlap and model the whole group of books with 70% or 80% accuracy. That won't necessarily prove that different readers agree. To get a more sensitive picture of the differences or similarities between readers, we will have to deliberately blind our model to some of the evidence and ask whether it can predict the judgments made by reader X using only evidence from reader Y.

Against Taxonomy

The word "genre" may evoke a mental image of a map that neatly partitions the landscape of fiction so that each work is located in one and only one region. Similar maps of musical genres have recently become popular online, and the rhetoric of supervised learning—with its references to "classification" and "accuracy"—may sound as though it begins from the assumption that cultural artifacts can be placed in a consistent taxonomy.[17] In fact, our descriptions of fiction haven't created any such map, nor have I attempted to produce one here. A novel like *The Woman in White* (1859) is assigned by some observers to "the Gothic" and by others to "the sensation novel." In my metadata it bears tags associated

17. Glenn McDonald, "Every Noise at Once," accessed March 12, 2018, http://everynoise.com/engenremap.html.

with both categories. If I found it in a bibliography of detective fiction, I would add a tag for that claim too, connected to the particular bibliography making the claim. There is no limit to the number of overlapping genre claims that can be associated with a single work.

Other novels aren't associated with any determinate genre at all. In reality most nineteenth-century fiction was categorized very loosely, perhaps only by the phrase "A Novel" printed on the title page. If we needed to produce a symmetrical taxonomy of genres, we might redress this embarrassing situation by assigning uncategorized nineteenth-century works to a loose grouping like "realism." But why assume that there is any consistent taxonomy underlying human opinion? Let's begin with the inconsistent evidence before us. Instead of postulating that a taxonomy must organize the literary landscape, we can ask, empirically, how far human acts of categorization actually agree with each other.

This chapter is accordingly organized as a series of questions about the compatibility of groups defined by different observers. We will start by asking whether one definition of "detective fiction" has much in common with another. If we're able to get consensus on that point, we'll ask whether the category of "detective fiction" can be stretched further to encompass crime fiction or the Newgate novel. In each case we'll assemble a set of works tagged with a particular group of genre claims and ask how well it can be distinguished from a contrast set of equal size. Usually the contrast set will be selected randomly from a digital library (except inasmuch as it excludes the tags that defined the positive set). The contrast set will also be distributed across time in a way that matches the distribution of the positive set as closely as possible.

If there is no difference between the two categories being compared, one would expect the model to fail, making predictions that are no better than random (50% accurate, since the sets are always the same size). And indeed, if we attempt to model the boundary between two genuinely random groups of books, we get a reassuring failure, no better than random guessing. But few categories produced by human selection are genuinely random. Even a very idiosyncratic or internally divided selection process will leave traces that can be modeled. For instance, if we mix works tagged as Gothic, detective, and science fiction, we produce a ghastly stew that few critics would call a coherent genre. But even this sprawling category can be distinguished from a random background, on average, 78% of the time. Glancing at a few of the most predictive features in the model—*murder, ghastly, lock, key, theory*, and *laboratory*—it is not hard to see how that happened. The genres involved here are not entirely dissimilar; a model can easily find sensational props or plot devices they have in common.

But genres occupy a space of similarity with more than three dimensions, so things that are very close along one axis can still be far apart in other ways. Although we can identify a mixture of detective, science fiction, and Gothic with 78% accuracy, the differences *between* these genres are even stronger than their collective difference from a randomly selected background. A model trained to distinguish detective fiction from the Gothic is right more than 93% of the time.

In other words, predictive models are rather like human beings: they can always find some ways two sets of works are similar and other ways they differ. If we want to know whether detective fiction and science fiction can be lumped together, no single model will answer the question. Instead, we need to pose a four-sided question that allows us to ask whether the differences defining one genre are parallel to the differences that define another. Do detective stories differ from other works of fiction *in the same way* that science fiction differs? To answer this question, one can train a model on the contrast between detective fiction and a randomly selected background and then ask the same model to distinguish works of science fiction from the same background. As we might expect, this model fails utterly: it's right less than half of the time. Although these two genres have a few things in common (theories and laboratories, for instance), their common elements seem not to be the features that most saliently define them. When I need to decide whether two models of genre are similar, in the pages that follow, this is the test I will trust. Since I run it in both directions (asking a model trained only on A to recognize B, and vice versa), I call it "the method of mutual recognition." This test certainly tells us that our ghastly "genre stew" can be separated out into detective fiction, science fiction, and the Gothic. The next question is whether "detective fiction" itself similarly breaks up into subgenres—groups of works linked by chronology or by a particular site of reception—that differ more than they resemble each other.

Detective Fiction

When researchers look for genres in their local library, they commonly rely on Library of Congress genre/form headings. These tags were applied to volumes by individual librarians and reflect tacit assumptions about genre held by many different people. They will provide an important source of evidence in this chapter. We can create an initial sample of detective fiction, for instance, by selecting works that librarians have tagged "Detective and mystery fiction." But as we go back before 1940, these tags become very sparse, because we're looking at books that were originally cataloged before the Library of Congress system assumed its present form. Only a few of those works have been recataloged in the last eighty years.

To create a sample of a genre from this earlier period we have to rely on bibliographies and critical studies. For pre–World War II detective fiction, I have relied on the catalog of an exhibition organized at Indiana University Library in 1973, covering "The First Hundred Years of Detective Fiction, 1841–1941."[18] This lists collections of short stories (and a few individual stories) along with novels. It also includes works in translation. I have been similarly inclusive throughout this chapter. Writers like

18. *The First Hundred Years of Detective Fiction, 1841–1941*, Lilly Library, Bloomington, IN, 1973, accessed 2015, http://www.indiana.edu/~liblilly/etexts/detective/.

Jules Verne and Émile Gaboriau strongly shaped the history of genre beyond France, so we would lose a lot by excluding them. I doubt, moreover, that there is anything untranslatable about the patterns detected by a model of genre: Verne will turn out to be an extremely typical figure within science fiction, even in translation.

It is of course possible that a single exhibition catalog of detective fiction (limited to volumes before 1941) will create a picture of the genre that diverges substantially from postwar volumes cataloged by many different hands. But that's exactly the kind of question statistical models allow us to test. Modeling just the eighty-eight volumes from the Indiana exhibition that I was able to obtain digitally, we have a rather high level of accuracy, 93.2%. The 194 volumes that have Library of Congress genre tags are more of a mixed bag and can only be recognized 91.0% of the time. If we combine both sets, we have 266 volumes (since 16 were in both groups) that can be recognized with 93.4% accuracy. So mixing groups selected in different ways doesn't reduce accuracy; it's a compromise that "levels upward."

But as I have mentioned, algorithmic models can be very good at finding common elements that link a group of works. A better way of comparing two human definitions of genre is to train a model on one reader's judgments and then ask it to predict judgments made by a different reader. For instance, when we ask a model trained on the Library of Congress detective fiction to distinguish the Indiana exhibition from a random background and vice versa, we still get 85% accuracy on average. That's the real confirmation that we're looking at largely congruent definitions of the detective story.

But what exactly *is* the definition of detective fiction operative in these models? It is not a shocking one. A quick glance at the words most predictive of detective fiction reveals the themes we would expect: *police, murder, investigation,* and *crime*. If we look a little deeper into the model, there are less obvious details. Architecture and domestic furnishing, for instance, loom large as a source of clues: *door, room, window,* and *desk* are all highly predictive words. On the opposite side of the model, words that describe childhood and education (*born, grew, taught, children*) strongly predict that a volume is not detective fiction. Perhaps the genre's focus on a particular mysterious incident (or its tendency to take short-story form) encourage a contraction of biographical horizons.

It would be easy to put too much emphasis on these details. A model with four thousand variables is likely to contain many overlapping patterns, and even after we sort variables by their importance in the model, the important patterns will not all be contained in a few legible features at the top of the list. For instance, if we restrict our model to one hundred extremely common words, we can still identify detective stories with 86% accuracy, without any references to police or crime. The predictive words in this version of the model include vaguely interrogative signals appropriate for mysteries—*who, why, any, something,* and the question mark—but also more puzzling words like *have* and *was.* In short, the models created by machine learning are not mysterious black boxes: it is quite possible to crack them open and ask how they work. But they work so well, in part, because they are under no obligation to condense the world into a crisp definition. A model of a complex, overdetermined concept is likely to be just as overdetermined itself. Working with a light touch, a critic who has read a few detective stories can use predictive features to tease out insights (the absence of children in these stories, for instance, is an interesting dog that didn't bark). But it would be a mistake to imagine that a predictive model can quickly resolve arguments about the essential features of a genre. For that kind of condensing, prioritizing work, we still need critical debate.

On the other hand, statistical models are very good at comparing different frames of reference, and a method of that kind may be exactly what we need to address the skepticism about continuity now prevailing in genre theory. We have already seen, for instance, that a model trained on detective stories before 1941 is almost equally good at recognizing a collection of postwar detective fiction. How far can we stretch that sort of continuity?

Suppose we divide the history of detective fiction at 1915, before pulp magazines and writers like Agatha Christie or Raymond Chandler are thought to have given the genre its modern form. Can a model trained only on writers like Poe and Arthur Conan Doyle still recognize post–World War I detective fiction? Yes, without much difficulty. A model trained on examples published before 1915 is still 84% accurate with examples published on or after that date, and a model trained on the later set is right 87.8% of the time about the pre–World War I genre. This doesn't imply that there was no change across the timeline. We know that a great deal changed: the hardboiled style, for instance, hadn't yet begun to emerge in 1914. We could certainly train a model that would distinguish earlier and later examples of the genre. So the historian's standard chestnut—that continuity can coexist with change—holds true here, as it does everywhere. But our inquiry hasn't been posing a vague question open to that standard answer. We have been asking, more specifically, "Do the differences *that distinguish detective stories from other works of fiction* change enough to make twentieth-century examples of the genre hard to recognize?" And the answer to that is straightforwardly no. The things added to the genre, like hardboiled style, never efface the genre's other differentiating features. Scholars like Maurizio Ascari, who argue that the contemporary genre has little to do with Poe, are simply not right.

The value of these methods is not just to affirm continuity. They are also sensitive enough to register discontinuity when it occurs. For instance, not every genealogy of detective fiction begins with Poe. Other influential arguments have traced the genre's concern with policing social order back to the Newgate novel of the 1830s or have found formal continuities with the sensation novels of the 1860s and 1870s.[19] There is doubtless something to both claims, but the continuities involved are weaker than the

19. D. A. Miller, *The Novel and the Police* (Berkeley: University of California Press, 1988); Christopher Pittard, "From Sensation to the Strand," in *A Companion to Crime Fiction*, ed. Charles J. Rzepka and Lee Horsley (Oxford: Wiley-Blackwell, 2010), 105–16.

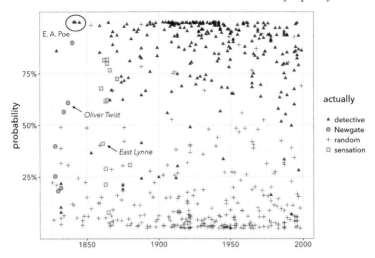

FIGURE 2.1. Probability of being detective fiction. Even when a model is trained on a definition of "detective fiction" that includes Newgate novels and sensation fiction, it tends to see those subgenres as outliers.

continuity with Poe. For instance, we can test these genres' similarity to other forms of detective fiction using the same method of mutual recognition we used to confirm continuity across the First and Second World Wars: in the case of the Newgate novel, this produces an accuracy of 59%, and for the sensation novel, 67.5%—distinctly lower than we found in earlier comparisons.[20] Alternatively, we can group all these genres into a single pool and ask which books turn out to be especially typical or especially hard to recognize. This question is easy to pose because statistical models naturally express their predictions as probabilities. So we can spread volumes out along a vertical axis that measures the model's degree of confidence that they belong to the positive set. In figure 2.1 I've done that with a model trained on 287 volumes from all the genres described above.

20. Keith Hollingsworth, *The Newgate Novel, 1830–1847: Bulwer, Ainsworth, Dickens and Thackeray* (Detroit: Wayne State University Press, 1963); Winifred Hughes, "The Sensation Novel," in *A Companion to the Victorian Novel*, ed. Patrick Brantlinger and William B. Thesing (Malden, MA: Blackwell, 2002), 260–78.

The model is very confident about most of the nineteenth- and twentieth-century volumes categorized as detective fiction. But it has difficulty recognizing Newgate and sensation novels as members of the same set, even though it has been trained on a sample that includes them and has not been given any indication that they are different from other detective stories. By contrast, Edgar Allan Poe's three short stories from the 1840s seem entirely consonant with later definitions of the genre. The patterns that link Sue Grafton to Arthur Conan Doyle extend backward all the way to Poe—but not much farther.

In short, quantitative methods are not inherently biased toward continuity or discontinuity. When cultural forms do change suddenly, a predictive model can recognize the break without being specifically instructed to do so. Of course, many scholars have already highlighted "The Murders in the Rue Morgue" as an important inflection point for crime fiction. Our model is not telling us anything radically new about Poe—in part, perhaps, because sudden innovations are things readers have always found easy to notice. But if we consider the other end of the timeline and compare the tight grouping of detective fiction from 1900 to 1949 to the more scattered pattern of detective fiction from 1950 to 1999, we may glimpse a more gradual change that has been harder to confirm on the scale of an individual reader's memory. It looks very much as if detective fiction is losing its crisp boundaries and starting to blur into other genres. This observation is made commonly enough about particular authors: Mercedes Lackey and Walter Mosley, for instance, both have a generic range that is difficult to pigeonhole. (And both authors do hover around the 50% mark in our model of detective fiction.) But when an argument is pinned to specific authors, it can be difficult to know whether the examples adduced are typical or exceptional. A model of 287 volumes puts us in a position to confirm that the similarities between works of detective fiction are really becoming looser, overall, in the 1990s than they were in the 1920s or 1930s.

The Gothic

The history of Gothic fiction creates, appropriately, a mystery about ancestral figures that haunt their descendants only as ambiguous traces. Critics seem fairly confident that the Gothic novel was a coherent phenomenon in Britain from 1760 to perhaps 1830. But as we move further into the nineteenth century, it becomes less and less clear whether the Gothic remains a continuous tradition. Franco Moretti divides the nineteenth-century Gothic into two genres at opposite ends of the century—the later one, which contains *Dracula*, designated "imperial Gothic." In twentieth-century America, "southern Gothic" is often treated as a distinct literary phenomenon. A specifically female Gothic tradition might run back through Du Maurier's *Rebecca* to Brontë's *Jane Eyre*. On the other hand, there are critical traditions that insist on the continuity of all these things and even stretch the Gothic to encompass the contemporary publishing category of "horror."

Since we have good reasons to wonder whether "the Gothic" writ large is a strongly unified tradition, it was particularly important in this case to compare different sources of testimony. Before 1840 I relied heavily on the Stanford Literary Lab's list of Gothic fiction; after 1840 I relied on the Library of Congress genre tags associated with "horror" or the "ghost story." But I also collected a set of works mentioned in *The Gothic*, a Blackwell guide edited by David Punter and Glennis Byron (2004), which traces a Gothic tradition all the way from Horace Walpole to Brett Easton Ellis, linked through a surprising range of intermediary figures that includes Emily Brontë, Henry James, and H. P. Lovecraft.

Few of these lists display the kind of coherence we found in detective fiction. The samples that can be predicted most accurately are the smallest: the twenty-one works (1791–1834) identified as Gothic by the Stanford Literary Lab can be recognized 86% of the time, and the twenty-seven volumes tagged "Ghost story" (1826–1920) can be recognized 91% of the time. The hardest sample to model is the superset that combines them all: 171 volumes that can only be modeled with 81.0% accuracy. The growing shakiness of this Gothic edifice as samples grow larger betrays a weakness somewhere in its foundation. In modeling a homogenous group of works, accuracy ordinarily increases as one gathers more data. That is what happened, for instance, with detective fiction. Declining accuracy suggests that our different sources are describing heterogenous things. We can confirm this using the method of mutual recognition. A model trained on Romantic-era Gothic works recognizes ghost stories only weakly and vice versa (69.8%); ghost stories are even less similar to twentieth-century horror (67.8%). If one compares twentieth-century horror directly to the Romantic-era Gothic, there is hardly any textual similarity at all (51.0%).

I don't expect this pattern to surprise many readers. Few critics claim that the Gothic is a genre as tightly knit as detective fiction. Even in the process of constructing a two-century anthology, Punter and Byron acknowledge the possibility that "there are very few actual literary texts which are 'Gothic'; that the Gothic is more do to with particular moments, tropes, repeated motifs that are found scattered . . . through modern western literary tradition."[21] Establishing that the Gothic falls apart is a test less of the Gothic than of our method. A method that didn't recognize hard cases would be hard to trust about others!

I have characterized the Gothic as an ancestral memory, but the weakness of this genre is not simply a consequence of the passage of time. It is true that our timeline for the Gothic stretches back 240 years, 80 years further than for detective fiction. But making the timelines equal wouldn't render the genres equally coherent: there is no 160-year segment of the Gothic timeline that displays anything like the kind of coherence we saw in the detective genre. For that matter, there is little evidence that the 160-year history of detective fiction makes it more diffuse

21. David Punter and Glennis Byron, *The Gothic* (Malden, MA: Blackwell, 2004), xviii.

than shorter-lived trends. A group of detective novels randomly selected from the entire 160-year timeline can be modeled just as accurately as an equal-sized group selected from 25 years of the genre or an equal-sized group of sensation novels drawn only from the 1860s and 1870s. Generation-sized genres are not more coherent than others. We may instinctively assume that cultural phenomena should grow more diffuse as they cover longer spans of time, but the evidence doesn't always bear this out.

The fractures within the Gothic are caused not just by time but by the genre's reliance on several distinct thematic premises: ghost stories, Romantic-era tales of incarceration and escape (often mixed with a courtship plot), and twentieth-century horror. Each of these things is easier to model on its own than in combination with the others. Detective fiction is not internally divided in quite the same way. There are, to be sure, subgenres of detective fiction. In the twentieth century, for instance, I have used bibliographies to separate hard-boiled detective novels (Raymond Chandler, Mickey Spillane) from the sort of mysteries set in a country house with a closed circle of known suspects (Agatha Christie, Margery Allingham).[22] A statistical model can easily distinguish these subgenres from each other: they are stylistically alien, in part because the hard-boiled style is histrionically gendered. Raymond Chandler openly defined the hard-boiled detective as a masculine (and American) response to the perceived femininity and intellectualism of British mysteries. But subgenres of detective fiction are never easier to model on their own than in combination. They can be at once very distinct (along a gendered stylistic axis) and very similar (along a different axis, which expresses a shared reliance on the criminal puzzle plot, in contrast to mainstream fiction).

In short, when we ask whether a genre is "unified," we are posing a complex question, which involves the depth and char-

22. John Charles, Joanna Morrison, and Candace Clark, *The Mystery Readers' Advisory: The Librarian's Clues to Murder and Mayhem* (Chicago: ALA, 2002); Geoffrey O'Brien, *Hardboiled America: Lurid Paperbacks and the Masters of Noir* (New York: Van Nostrand Reinhold, 1981).

acter of its internal divisions, as well as the extent of change over time. It is not safe to assume that all genres change at the same pace or that the existence of distinct subgenres will necessarily weaken a parent category. In the case of the Gothic, the forces of drift and division do work against coalescence. But even so, the term names a real phenomenon: a group of texts that can be recognized with 81% accuracy over a span of 240 years can hardly be called inchoate. Critics sometimes acknowledge the contrast with more tightly unified literary groups by calling the Gothic a mode rather than a genre. The term is fair enough, but like many terminological distinctions, it substitutes a crisp binary division for a more muddled reality. In the next section of this chapter, we will look at an intermediate case where the question of unity is not so easily resolved.

Science Fiction

I have argued that genre concepts that persist for more than a century can be just as coherent, linguistically, as those that persist for a few decades. But so far detective fiction is my only example, and there are reasons to suspect that the detective/mystery/crime genre might rely on an unusually stable set of premises. There's always a crime; there's always a detective; there's always an investigation. Science fiction would appear to pose a more challenging problem, because the premises of the genre are inherently mutable. The prototypes of the genre often describe conveyances like balloons and submarines that are no longer science fictional. Recent examples depend on information technology, which may produce a rather different plot. It is not immediately obvious that William Gibson's *Neuromancer* would share much common vocabulary with Verne's *Twenty Thousand Leagues under the Sea.* Many skeptical theories of genre have taken shape specifically around the mutability of science fiction—as the article "There Is No Such Thing as Science Fiction" reminds us.[23] In short, it

23. Vint and Bould, "There Is No Such Thing as Science Fiction"; see also Kincaid, "On the Origins of Genre"; Rieder, "On Defining SF."

is not intuitively clear whether we should expect science fiction to hold together over long timelines, like detective fiction, or fall apart like the Gothic.

Since there are different stories about the early history of science fiction, I drew on several different sources for that period. *The Anatomy of Wonder* is a well-known bibliography with chapters on early science fiction contributed by Brian Stableford, a writer of science fiction himself. Stableford's history of the genre strongly emphasizes H. G. Wells and the future-war tradition but is somewhat more reticent about other predecessor figures, like Mary Shelley and Jane Loudon. (Like many historians of science fiction, Stableford tends to define the genre through its scientific content, and he can be skeptical about works where that content seems lacking.) To get a fuller representation of women in the genre, I relied on a bibliography of women in early science fiction constructed by Mary Mark Ockerbloom. In spite of their different emphases, these sources construct lists of texts that can be modeled in very similar ways.[24]

When all these bibliographic sources are folded together, we have a list of 213 volumes stretching from 1771 to 1999 that can be modeled with 90.6% accuracy. The boundaries of this genre are a little less clear than detective fiction, but it certainly has a coherence more akin to that genre than to the Gothic.

The scientific romances of the late nineteenth century are often described as groping toward a concept of genre that had not yet fully crystallized. But the model in figure 2.2 has no difficulty recognizing them as akin to Ursula Le Guin and cyberpunk. Three books by Jules Verne are all assigned to science fiction with a greater than 99% probability. Mary Shelley is a more ambiguous case. Her apocalyptic plague story, *The Last Man* (1826), is recognized confidently as science fiction, but *Frankenstein* (1818)

24. Brian Stableford, "The Emergence of Science Fiction, 1516–1914," and "Science Fiction between the Wars, 1918–1938," in *Anatomy of Wonder: A Critical Guide to Science Fiction*, ed. Neil Barron, 5th ed. (Santa Barbara, CA: Libraries Unlimited, 2004), 3–22, 23–44; Mary Mark Ockerbloom, "Pre-1950 Utopias and Science Fiction by Women: An Annotated Reading List of Online Editions," accessed 2015, http://digital.library.upenn .edu/women/_collections/utopias/utopias.html.

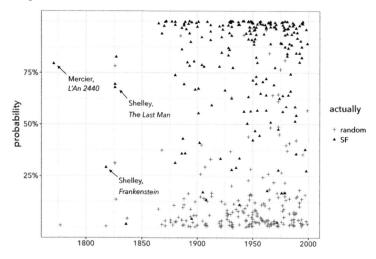

FIGURE 2.2. Probability of being science fiction. Science fiction, 1771–1999, classified with 90.6% accuracy.

hovers around the middle of the spectrum—as it does, frankly, in much critical commentary on the genre. So the boundaries of science fiction do become blurrier as we move back before Verne. Another site of ambiguity (not explored in figure 2.2) is the porous boundary between science fiction and fantasy. I have deferred that complex topic to a future article. Here it may suffice to say that science fiction and fantasy are separable traditions but traditions that have long been closely connected (more closely than either is connected to other genres).

Our list of science fiction, assembled by many different hands, includes cosmic evolutionary histories (Olaf Stapledon's *Last and First Men*) and personal dream visions (Marie Corelli's *A Romance of Two Worlds*); voyages into the future (Louis Mercier's *L'An 2440*), and into a prehistoric past (Arthur Conan Doyle's *The Lost World*). How is it possible to model such a long and varied tradition just by counting words? Science fiction turns out to have a strong stylistic signature, which we might loosely characterize as sublime. Invocations of scale (*vast, far, larger, infinite*) are very characteristic of the genre, as are large numbers (*thousands*, *millions*). *Horror*, *nightmare*, and *destruction* are more prominent than one might have imagined. Self-conscious references to the *human* tend to accompany *creatures* against which *humanity* may be defined, and the pronoun *its* is common, since we often confront *unknown things* that lack an easily recognized human gender. At the other end of the scale, a whole range of quotidian details mark a book as probably not science fiction: references to *tea* or a *hat*, for instance, and to particular days of the week.

This is not by any means an exhaustive description of the model, and I want to be careful not to imply that sublime estrangement, by itself, is a sufficient definition of science fiction. This is just one salient and widely shared aspect of the genre's style. But this angle of analysis may help us understand why Mary Shelley's apocalyptic intensity belongs in our history of science fiction, with or without detailed scientific content. The same thing might be said about some of the randomly selected books that the model strongly (and persuasively) misclassifies as science fiction, like Thomas Pynchon's *Crying of Lot 49* and William S. Burroughs's *The Ticket That Exploded*. It may not be Pynchon's explicit concern with entropy but his paranoid fascination with the sheer scale of mass society that this model sees as connected to the tradition of science fiction.

One thing we might expect that doesn't appear in the model is the gradual consolidation of genre conventions that science fiction scholars spend so much time tracing. Historians of this genre are rarely as willing to give Verne as much credit as historians of detective fiction give Poe. The narrative premise of much historiography is that science fiction was an inchoate phenomenon (scattered across utopias, planetary romances, future-war narratives, and so on) until given a new shape and direction by particular American pulp magazines and anthologies between 1925 and 1950. Hugo Gernsback's *Amazing Stories* (1926) often plays a central role. Gary Wolfe says, for instance, that "science fiction, despite its healthy legacy throughout the nineteenth century, was essentially a *designed* genre after 1926." Even after that point, "the science fiction novel persistently failed to cohere as a genre in the manner of mysteries and Westerns" until *The Pocket Book of Science Fiction* emerged in 1943.[25]

As we will see in a moment, Wolfe and other scholars are probably right that science fiction changed rapidly in the middle of the twentieth century. But claims about failure to cohere are another matter: I don't find much evidence to support them. The scientific romances of the late nineteenth and early twentieth century (1850–1925) seem to cohere perfectly well—in the sense that they resemble each other as closely and can be modeled almost as accurately (88.9%) as later examples of "science fiction" (90.2%). It is true that these ties of similarity are not quite as strong as the conventions organizing prewar detective fiction, but then, science fiction never becomes quite as predictable as detective fiction. I think one has to conclude that the early history of this genre looks incoherent to our retrospective gaze for parochial, presentist reasons. For instance, we are probably giving too much weight to the term *science fiction* itself, to the plausible scientific content that Gernsback demanded from his writers, and to a particular set of postwar technologies that we have come to view as iconic (robotics, spaceflight).

One could, admittedly, object that my list of nineteenth-century scientific romances comes mostly from twentieth-century histories of science fiction. Perhaps this group of texts is only coherent because it was selected, tacitly, to provide a set of precursors for a more strongly unified genre? This is a fair objection. In some cases this chapter has been able to found genre categories on nineteenth-century evidence: informal lists of Newgate novels and sensation novels, for instance, were constructed by reviewers at the time. But "scientific romance" was a looser category in the nineteenth century. Although the term was widely applied to Verne, Camille Flammarion, and H. G. Wells, I haven't found a bibliography or reading list that I could use as strictly contemporary evidence for the boundaries of the genre. So there may

25. Wolfe, *Evaporating Genres*, 34, 21.

be something retrospective about the lists of nineteenth-century science fiction used here. But it is still significant that the concept coheres on a textual level. There is no way to construct the same kind of retrospective coherence for the Gothic.

If received stories about the incoherence of pre–pulp science fiction are misleading, is there, at least, some evidence that the pulps made a difference in the genre? Yes, there is, but measuring the pace of generic change is tricky. It might be tempting simply to measure the linguistic distance between science fiction in the 1920s and in the 1960s. But a simple measurement of distance risks conflating different questions. We wouldn't want a broadly shared change in diction (say, the rise of contractions) to count as a change specific to science fiction. Instead, we need evidence that the distinguishing characteristics of the genre itself altered.

We can measure this sort of change by adapting the method of mutual recognition described earlier in this chapter. Sliding a window of sixty years down the length of a timeline, we can, first, model each thirty-year half of the window on its own, making generic predictions about works using contemporary evidence. Then we can switch the models: make predictions about 1930–59 using a model developed in 1900–29 and vice versa. Usually these predictions will be less accurate than the predictions that used immediately contemporary evidence. The amount of accuracy lost across any given midpoint (e.g., 1930 in our example) will give us one way to assess the pace of generic change across the whole sixty-year window.

In the case of science fiction, I think the story suggested in figure 2.3 matches received histories of the genre reasonably well. There are five lines for each genre because I ran the test five times, using a different randomly selected 85% of the books each time. For science fiction, the pace of change always peaks between 1930 and 1950, in a period that loosely aligns with Wolfe's narrative of consolidation, bookended by the emergence of *Amazing Stories* in 1926 and the *Pocket Book of Science Fiction* in 1943. Detective fiction does not show the same midcentury acceleration of change—which is important, because it adds confidence that the

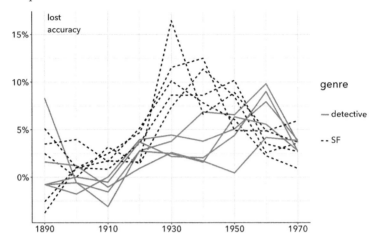

FIGURE 2.3. Pace of change in detective fiction and science fiction. Change is measured as the loss of accuracy when we use thirty years of the past to predict the future, and vice versa, compared to accuracy when each period makes predictions about itself.

shift is not produced by any purely mechanical change in our corpus (for instance, by changing the source of volumes from HathiTrust to the Chicago Text Lab at 1923). Moreover, I have recently replicated this experiment using a different set of volumes, drawn entirely from HathiTrust, and 1940 still turns up as the peak of change in science fiction.

So if science fiction did change rapidly between 1930 and 1950, what kind of change are we detecting? This doesn't have to be a mysterious question; there are many ways to open the so-called black box of machine learning and find answers. For instance, one way to locate change is to ask which later books are hard for models trained on an earlier period to recognize. Since models assign each book a probability of being science fiction, we can simply compare the probabilities assigned by models trained on different periods. This produces a measure of historical parallax or, so to speak, of surprise. If we sort science fiction in the period 1940–75 by this measure, clear patterns emerge. First, prewar models tend to be surprised by books of science fiction written by women or with women as protagonists. Books by Catherine Lucile Moore and Ursula Le Guin are near the top of the list, along with Samuel Delany's *Babel-17* (with its protagonist Rydra Wong). But gender itself doesn't seem to be the full story: prewar models are just as surprised by Philip K. Dick and by Robert Heinlein's *Stranger in a Strange Land*.

If we wonder which particular aspects of these books stretched earlier conceptions of science fiction, we can pose the question by allowing different models to read brief passages. Then we can sort passages by the size of the difference between predictions made by prewar and postwar models. Many of the passages where the models disagree most sharply have a psychological or social dimension. The following example from *Babel-17* is typical. (I have italicized words that make prewar models particularly skeptical that this is science fiction.)

> What "self"? There was no "I."
>
> She had entered him in some bewildering reversed sexuality. Enclosing her, he was in agony. The light—you make! You make! his *crying* in terror.
>
> Butcher, she asked, more familiar in patterning words about *emotional* turbulences than he, what does my mind in yours look like?
>
> *Bright, bright* moving, he howled, the analytical *precision* of Babel-17, *crude* as stone to articulate their melding, making so many *patterns*, re-*forming* them.[26]

There is a lot going on in this passage. Our model may not necessarily notice, for instance, that Delany has distorted English syntax to reflect his characters' struggle to communicate. The model does notice, however, that the central conflict of the passage is psychological: words like *emotional* and *crying* are legible clues, and they do a lot to convince models trained on prewar evidence that this passage is not science fiction. The passages of Le Guin's *Left Hand of Darkness* that are hardest for prewar models to recognize as science fiction similarly explore the psychological and social consequences of alien sexuality. And although Robert Heinlein's

26. Samuel R. Delany, *Babel-17* (London: Victor Gollancz, 1967), 159–60.

politics were different from Delany's and Le Guin's, *Stranger in a Strange Land* fails to fit prewar models of science fiction for the same reason: it pays less attention to the physics of spaceflight than to psychological, social (and specifically sexual) disorientation. Arthur C. Clarke, by contrast, is relatively easy for early-twentieth-century models to recognize as a science fiction writer.

Critics of quantitative approaches to culture often worry, with Martin Jay, that "there is no easy passage from micro- to macroanalysis."[27] That might be true, if macroanalysis meant simply counting words (as Jay assumes). A graph of macroscopic trends in word frequency can't tell us how the trend might have been produced by changes in individual books or paragraphs. But a predictive model of genre is another matter. Models are inherently relational, and one of their strengths is to build bridges between different scales of analysis—allowing us to understand how the historical contrast between two periods was expressed at the scale of the paragraph. I doubt the conclusions I have just drawn about *Babel-17* will surprise scholars of science fiction; the new centrality of psychological conflict in the 1960s loosely aligns with the well-known emergence of a New Wave in the genre. But this chapter's conclusions about long-term generic coherence and change are less obvious, and I felt it was important to show how those generalizations could be anchored in the recognizable stylistic quirks of individual paragraphs. Once we have a model of genre, that connection is not difficult to build.

In short, the so-called Golden Age of science fiction does seem to have been associated with an acceleration of change; works before that period are significantly different from the works published afterward. What isn't borne out is the common assumption that scientific romance before the pulp era was less coherent: a mere hodgepodge of literary premises struggling to coalesce around the genre concept that would eventually give them meaning. Nineteenth-century scientific romance may not

27. Martin Jay, "'Hey! What's the Big Idea?': Ruminations on the Question of Scale in Intellectual History," *New Literary History* 48, no. 4 (2017): 626.

have had the institutional solidity or brand identity that science fiction later acquired. But our habit of equating brand identity with literary consolidation seems not to be well founded. The varied premises of late-nineteenth-century dream visions, voyages, and planetary romances don't prevent them from resembling each other, textually, as strongly as Golden Age works of science fiction. And although change did accelerate in the middle of the twentieth century, the changes in science fiction were never dramatic enough to prevent us from modeling two hundred years of the genre as a single unit.

Statistical Models and Genre Theory

The evidence gathered in this chapter challenges three existing theories of genre. Franco Moretti's conjecture that genre is a generational cycle is probably the least important of these targets: Moretti offered it as a reluctant speculation, and it has only been adopted by a few other scholars.[28] In any case, I have found no evidence to support it. The premise that genre boundaries gradually "consolidate" in the early twentieth century is a more serious matter. The notion that the pulps gave form to protean traditions that had previously "failed to cohere" is very influential in science fiction criticism.[29] But as we have seen above, the distinctive language of science fiction seems to take form before the institutions that are supposed to have consolidated it. The third theory of genre I have questioned is the recently popular notion that histories of genre are merely a genealogical thread linking a flux of disparate cultural forms. Predictive models can directly challenge this claim. If a model trained on detective fiction before 1914 can also recognize detective (and crime) fiction after that date, then then the differences separating the genre from the rest of the literary field must have remained relatively stable.

28. Adam Roberts, "A Brief Note on Moretti and Science Fiction," in *Reading Graphs, Maps, Trees: Critical Responses to Franco Moretti*, ed. Jonathan Goodwin and John Holbo (Anderson, SC: Parlor, 2011), 49–55.

29. Wolfe, *Evaporating Genres*, 21.

The historical picture that emerges from this inquiry is not simple. At first glance, there is a fairly clear contrast between long-lived twentieth-century genres (detective fiction and science fiction) and shorter-lived nineteenth-century phenomena (the Newgate novel or sensation fiction). But the rationale for this contrast is far from clear. Detective fiction and science fiction both seem to have stabilized before the modern marketing institutions that are usually offered to explain their stability. For that matter, it is not clear why certain genres stabilize more than others. Gothic novels and science fiction can both be traced back to the eighteenth century. It is not intuitively obvious why science fiction should have turned out to be the less mutable member of that pair.

In short, this chapter leaves many questions open. Its provisional conclusions could be revised by improving models or by adding perspectives from a wider range of observers. But even these tentative conclusions reveal that statistical models can challenge literary scholars' assumptions about the history of genre. Moreover, I hope it is beginning to become clear that the limitations of a quantitative approach lie in a different place than popular notions about mathematics might suggest.

Numbers are widely associated with a quest for objectivity in the physical sciences. In this story, the scientist is imagined to approach the world like Sherlock Holmes, "with an absolutely blank mind . . . simply . . . to observe and to draw inferences from our observations."[30] Humanists, for their part, have grown proud of unsettling that claim to objectivity. So any suggestion that numbers might illuminate human history immediately calls forth a well-rehearsed script, where math is expected to define objective patterns and humanists sigh that things are more complicated and depend on the observer's assumptions.

This script is rooted in years of conflict over the social role of natural science—in an era when numbers were good for mea-

---

30. Arthur Conan Doyle, "The Adventure of the Cardboard Box," in *His Last Bow: A Reminiscence of Sherlock Holmes* (New York: Review of Reviews, 1917), 82.

suring physical things but almost useless for modeling human perspectives. Mathematical models that depend on social context may force us to reconsider the whole script. Numbers would do little to help someone who really approached the world, like Holmes, with an absolutely blank mind. If you want to count sheep, someone has to point at an animal first and say "that's a sheep." Similarly, to model genres I had to consult historically situated observers who pointed at Jules Verne and Samuel Delany, Agatha Christie and Raymond Chandler. Numbers did nothing to make this inquiry less perspectival. But they did allow us to compare perspectives and describe differences of degree between them. Once various observers have provided examples of the Gothic, for instance, we can use mathematical models to ask how compatible their assumptions are or how rapidly the genre mutates as we move down a timeline. In short, the point of quantification can be to render description relative rather than objective. Perspectival models are deeply compatible with an antifoundational approach to interpretation.

The Long Arc of Prestige

So far, this book has emphasized the history of genres, themes, and narrative devices. In short, it has mainly been a history of things that happen between the covers of a book.

Textual forms are important aspects of literary pleasure: there is no reason to apologize for studying them. But they are not the only part of history that can be enriched by quantitative reasoning. Until recently, in fact, numbers were far more useful for social questions than for aesthetic ones. Unemployment, inequality, and book sales are easy to measure. But it is not intuitively obvious how one would measure literary style. In making it possible to construct quantitative models of genres and styles, machine learning has made it easier to link formal concepts to quantitative social evidence and thus to build bridges between social history and the history of texts.

The preceding chapter has already provided one glimpse of the way such a bridge might work. Although genre can be understood as a formal concept, predictive modeling allowed us to investigate genre by posing questions that were less about the texts themselves than about the agreement uniting or separating different groups of readers. This chapter will similarly train models that use textual evidence to predict readers' responses to literary works. But where the preceding chapter uses that method to model genre, this chapter models literary prestige. Uniting social and textual evidence in a single model will allow us to make progress on questions where critics have often had to content themselves with speculation. How do the standards of literary distinction change? How rapidly? And how are the directions of literary change related to the social pressures exerted by reviewers or purchasers?

When I say that critics have contented themselves with speculation on these questions, I don't mean that we have been timid. Our speculations are often quite bold. With a charismatic sweep of the hand, we explain postmodernism as a consequence of late capitalism or say that Romanticism expresses the individualism of an ascendant bourgeoisie. But we don't expect flourishes of that kind to create much consensus. It is difficult to prove that abstract concepts spanning several decades have explanatory force. Critics have fiercely debated whether Romanticism, for instance, even exists.[1] So when historians are trying to produce consensus about cultural change, we tend to shift into a more cautious narrative mode emphasizing individual events: the construction of the Westin Bonaventure Hotel or the publication of *Lyrical Ballads*. Then we hope that readers will accept these events as emblems of a larger concept whose outlines we cannot sketch precisely.

The thesis of this chapter is that a different kind of description is possible, which will combine the rigor of a detailed account with the ambitious scope of a larger narrative. When we train a model using social and textual evidence across a whole century, we can describe long-term patterns that connect social pressures to persistent directions of literary change. This doesn't make shorter-term trends unimportant, but it puts them in a different perspective. Imagine if we could show, for instance, that food had been getting steadily spicier in the United States for the past century and that the best-reviewed restaurants had consis-

1. A. O. Lovejoy, "On the Discrimination of Romanticisms," *PMLA* 39 (1924): 229–53.

tently occupied the leading edge of this trend. The stories we tell about decade-long culinary trends might still be true. But those stories would also have to be seen as parts of a broader pattern, which would become central to any explanation of long-term culinary change. I don't know that this is true about American food. In fact, it seems unlikely. But this chapter argues that something analogous is true about English-language poetry and fiction between 1820 and 1949. Our received narrative of this period is organized by a succession of discrete concepts defining different criteria of judgment: Romanticism, Victorian realism, aestheticism, naturalism, and modernism. For many observers, this has implied a fairly profound transformation of literary opinion every generation or so. Modernism, for instance, was a "literary revolution" that changed not only how writers created new works but how they evaluated the past, producing "a radical and wholesale revision of the inherited conception of English literature."[2]

In fact, when we model the textual dimension of literary success, we find standards of judgment that change only gradually and slowly. A model trained on mid-nineteenth-century evidence can do a decent job of predicting which books will be prominent in the 1920s or 1930s. When standards do change, they can move in a consistent direction for a century at a time. This is not to say that shorter-lived concepts like "modernism" or "naturalism" are unimportant. But it is not safe to assume that long-term change is produced simply by stringing together the smaller generational conflicts that we spend so much time discussing. Instead, long arcs of change seem to be driven in significant measure by shared assumptions that rarely became overt subjects of debate.

This is not a pattern I expected to find. The work that eventually produced this chapter started as a collaborative project with Jordan Sellers, aimed at measuring differences between smaller

2. Chris Baldick, "Modernist Criticism and the English Literary Canon," in *Modernity, Modernism, Postmodernism*, ed. Manuel Barbeito (Santiago de Compostela, Spain: Universidad de Santiago de Compostela, 2000), 151–52.

slices of time. We hoped to trace the emergence of Andreas Huyssen's "great divide"—a widening gulf between mass culture and elite literary taste, which Huyssen describes as an emergent subject of concern in "the last decades of the 19th century and the first few years of the 20th."[3] The premise of our inquiry was that the stylistic differentiation caused by a widening social gulf should make literary prestige easier to model. A model of prestige in the middle of the nineteenth century might not be very accurate, because elite and popular culture wouldn't have hardened yet into two distinct idioms. But as an avant-garde consolidated and broke away from the mainstream, we expected that it would become easier and easier to detect social stratification at the level of diction. With that hypothesis in mind, we gathered evidence about four twenty-year slices of time between 1840 and 1920. The whole plan of the experiment was based on our assumption that standards of judgment might change significantly every twenty years.

We discovered patterns on a very different scale. It was certainly possible to model prestige in each twenty-year period. But our model of prestige became even more accurate when we folded the periods together and treated the whole eighty-year span as a single unit. Whatever changes happened across these eighty years, they apparently weren't profound enough to shake the underlying association between social prominence and particular kinds of literary language. Puzzled by this, we extended our study of poetry back to 1820. A subsequent collaboration with Jessica Mercado and Sabrina Lee stretched the timeline (for fiction) forward to 1950. In this chapter, I present an overview of all this evidence (with deep gratitude to all the collaborators who helped gather it). The big picture is that a stylistic stratification of literature is already clear in the middle of the nineteenth century and then remains fairly stable through the middle of the twentieth.

We did, in the end, discover evidence of the growing social

3. Huyssen, *After the Great Divide*, viii.

stratification that Andreas Huyssen and other historians have described. Broadly, our results confirm a version of this story often advanced by scholars of the Victorian era, which has portrayed this process less as a cultural division than as a gradual expansion of the reading audience, leading to a slow diversification of the market across three-decker novels, penny dreadfuls, yellowbacks, pulp magazines, and so on.[4] This may be slightly different from the darker and more dichotomous story of a great divide advanced by modernists and scholars of modernism, but it is not a radically new picture.

The more provocative parts of this chapter, I think, are things found by accident along the way. It is not just social stratification that changes slowly: the criteria of literary judgment themselves seem to be remarkably stable. When they do change, they move with the momentum of an ocean liner: an observer in the year 1900, equipped with a computer, could have predicted a significant component of change for the next fifty years just by extrapolating the directions of change visible in the last fifty. Literature seems to move in the direction of prestigious examples, and it can keep moving in roughly the same direction across a long timeline.

Shorter wavelengths of change matter too. In fact, anything readers have believed to be important is by definition important, because readers create literary significance. Critical perception is in that sense self-authorizing: the inherent significance of "naturalism" and "modernism" doesn't need to be confirmed by any measurement. But the scale of a given change in relation to prevailing social standards is a topic where our eyes can deceive us. We are not particularly good at taking in or remembering a whole century of literary reception at once, and our impressions of the past are often shaped by participants who had an interest in exaggerating the pivotal character of their own contributions. For that matter, our own interests as historians are often best served by dramatic narratives of conflict leading to a

---

4. Richard D. Altick, *The English Common Reader: A Social History of the Mass Reading Public, 1800–1900* (Chicago: University of Chicago Press, 1957).

"literary revolution" that conveniently bounds and organizes our manuscript. Comparison across a long timeline won't make any of these changes unimportant, but it can, I think, revise our sense of their relative proportions. Changes we have characterized as sudden revolutions may come to look more like eddies on the surface of a stream that was flowing all the time in a consistent direction.

The Plan of the Experiment

There are many ways to measure literary prestige. In the twentieth century, one might collect works that won prizes or those widely studied in schools. To be sure, not everyone will be satisfied by those definitions of prestige. Prizewinning works are not always thought to represent the true cutting edge; adoption in schools may come long after the peak of a work's celebrity.[5] But failure to satisfy everyone is exactly what we should expect from a measure of prestige, since prestige is a contested perspectival category. Eventually, we should identify celebrated works in many different ways and compare all of those subsets to understand how literature is valued differently in different social locations.

This chapter, however, is trying to chart prestige across a timeline that stretches from the nineteenth century into the twentieth. Literary prizes and school adoption won't make much sense as a measure of a novel's success in 1860; the novel form itself simply hadn't achieved that kind of consecration yet. So I have modeled literary prestige instead as the probability that an author will be discussed in certain elite periodicals. The assumption underlying this model is that being reviewed indicates a sort of literary distinction, even if your book is panned.

Scholars more commonly study reception by contrasting positive and negative reviews—an approach that makes sense if one

---

5. For the ambiguous status of nineteenth-century prizes, see James F. English, *The Economy of Prestige: Prizes, Awards, and the Circulation of Cultural Value* (Cambridge, MA: Harvard University Press, 2005), 28–49.

is interested in gradations of approval but that leaves out many works never reviewed at all in selective venues. This blind spot matters: literary historians cannot understand the boundaries of literary distinction if we only look at works on one side of the boundary. So although the team gathering evidence for this project recorded reviewers' sentiments when they were clear, we didn't in the end make extensive use of that evidence. Our fundamental criterion of prestige was the fact that an author got reviewed at all.

To make this strategy work, we needed to focus on periodicals that were selective about what they did review—usually quarterly, monthly, or fortnightly publications rather than weeklies. I created an initial list of titles by quizzing friends who are scholars of this period. Then I winnowed that list, in collaboration with several research assistants, by choosing journals that seemed especially selective in their literary reviewing.[6] For instance, the *Athenaeum* was influential but reviewed so many novels that it's not a sign of great distinction to be included there. Journals like the *Fortnightly Review*, with broadly intellectual ambitions, covered new fiction and poetry less often. Eminently good or eminently bad, literature reviewed there was at least marked as important.

We sampled poetry from 1820 to 1919 and fiction from 1850 to 1949, giving us two centuries, offset by thirty years but overlapping for seventy years in the middle. The periodicals used in the current study are listed in table 3.1. For each periodical, we have listed the earliest and latest year we sampled reviews and the numbers of volumes of poetry and fiction sampled.

We also needed a sample that would contain books reviewed less often. To confirm that a given book was never reviewed in any of these publications would have been a tedious task. It was easier simply to select works at random from a very large collec-

6. Jordan Sellers, Sabrina Lee, and Jessica Mercado made crucial historical decisions here. We relied on advice especially from Nina Baym, Ryan Cordell, Eleanor Courtemanche, Jeff Drouin, Andrew Gaedtke, Lauren Goodlad, Matthew Hart, Deanna Kreisel, Bethany Nowviskie, Anthony Mandal, Bruce Michelson, Justine Murison, and Roger Whitson.

TABLE 3.1. Periodicals used to construct a reviewed sample

Title	Date range	Vols. poetry	Vols. fiction
The Adelphi	1923–1949	0	11
The Atlantic	1859–1949	122	197
Blackwood's Magazine	1841–1996	16	71
The Crisis	1922–1938	0	6
The Criterion	1924–1939	0	12
The Dial	1921–1927	0	5
Dublin Magazine	1930–1949	0	10
Edinburgh Review	1820–1859	36	18
The Egotist	1914–1919	17	9
Fortnightly Review	1865–1914	59	102
Horizon	1940–1946	0	5
Graham's Magazine	1840–1856	19	0
The Little Review	1914–1915	0	3
Macmillan's Magazine	1880–1884	2	4
The New Age	1907–1920	2	19
The New Republic	1915–1947	0	33
The New Yorker	1925–1947	0	17
Poetry: A Magazine of Verse	1910–1916	32	0
Quarterly Review	1820–1857	20	3
The Savoy	1896	2	0
Scrutiny	1940–1946	0	3
Tait's Edinburgh Magazine	1852–1859	0	33
The Westminster Review	1842–1867	29	0
The Yale Review	1930–1949	0	16
The Yellow Book	1895–1896	2	7

tion, while excluding authors already in the reviewed sample. In practice, this turns up mostly books that were rarely reviewed. But because sampling was genuinely random, there will be a few well-known authors in the random sample. The model often recognizes these people and predicts that they will be successful— which sadly has to be counted against it as an "error." The random sample was selected from HathiTrust Digital Library, which contains the aggregated collections of large public and university libraries, producing a collection of several million books in English, of which about 112,600 include fiction (1850–1949) and about 56,700 include poetry (1820–1919).[7] A digital library is itself a sample, with particular selection biases, to be discussed below.

7. Ted Underwood, "Page-Level Genre Metadata for English-Language Volumes in HathiTrust, 1700–1922," figshare, last modified 2014, http://dx.doi.org/10.6084/m9 .figshare.1279201.

But it samples a social range much broader than the range covered by elite periodicals, and what I needed in this study was not completeness but contrast.

Models of Reception in Poetry and Fiction

To understand the transformation of literary standards, this chapter models a relationship between literary language and reception. What kinds of books succeed in a given era? How easy is it to recognize them, and how rapidly do their characteristics change?

Modeling genre, in chapter 2, was a relatively easy task. Genres are expressed on the surface of a literary text. Some genre concepts are blurry, but many are easy to recognize. In the easy cases, as we have seen, statistical models can reproduce human judgment with accuracy above 90%. The qualities that lead to literary success, by contrast, are hard even for human readers to identify. This should be no surprise. If distinction were easy to define, every writer would be free to write the same way, and the original basis for distinction would quickly evaporate. So the characteristics of a prestigious style are elusive by definition.

However, the methods that work best to model prestige are essentially the same methods used in chapter 2 to model genre. See appendix B for details of the method, but in brief: I considered works of poetry and fiction at the volume level (stripping front and back matter, algorithmically, to leave only the body text). Each volume was represented for the most part as a bag of words—simply counting the number of times each word occurred in the text. Before settling on this representation, I tried many other features (including rhyme and meter for poetry and "conditional entropy" for fiction). But clever additions of that kind didn't improve the models significantly, and tiny increases in predictive accuracy are rarely worth large increases in complexity. Better methods of predicting literary success will no doubt eventually emerge. Jodie Archer and Matthew L. Jockers, for instance, recently published a popular book that argues that explicit

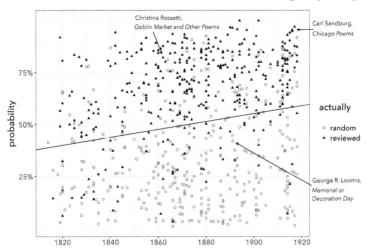

FIGURE 3.1. Probability of belonging to reviewed poetry set. A model of prestige in American and British poetry, 1820–1919, achieving 79.5% accuracy. The trend line is a linear regression on the points plotted.

representations of plot and character improve a model's ability to predict best sellers.[8] But the authors don't specify how much difference those factors made or share code and data, so at this point it is impossible to draw firm conclusions from their argument.

In any event, where poetry is concerned, prestige is not as difficult to model as one might assume. As one can see in figure 3.1, a model based on diction does a reasonable job of sorting reviewed from random works—and can do so for the whole century at once. Each of the points in this graph is a volume of poems; the circles are randomly selected, and the triangles are selected from reviews. The vertical placement of each volume indicates the model's confidence that it came from the reviewed sample. We can evaluate the model using the flat 50% line in the middle of the vertical axis. The model places 79.5% of the volumes on the right side of the dividing line, and since there are equal numbers

8. Jodie Archer and Matthew L. Jockers, *The Bestseller Code: Anatomy of the Blockbuster Novel* (New York: St. Martin's, 2016), 73–111, 147–82.

of volumes in both categories, this simple measure is an adequate measure of the model's accuracy. Four out of five times, we can predict the reception a book of poems will get just by looking at the text.

If one looks closely at the corners of figure 3.1, a subtle skew will become visible. On average, the points representing volumes drift upward slightly over time. The slanted regression line indicates the slope of change. Technically, this upward drift is an error in the model. Volumes are not really more likely to be reviewed just because they were published later: the reviewed and random volumes have the same distribution across the timeline. But this is an error of an interesting sort. A model trying to predict success for the whole century fails to produce perfectly evenhanded criteria, because books published later tend to have more of the verbal signals associated with success (across the whole century). This upward drift suggests that historical change across the timeline moved in the direction of the standards that governed reception at any given point on the timeline.

Before drawing any inferences from that interesting detail, I want to reflect for a moment on the significance of the fact that this model works at all. It isn't self-evident that we should be able to guess whether a book of poems will be reviewed purely by looking at the text. Genres influence the creation of a literary work, and it is not surprising that they leave textual traces. But here we are predicting an event that would have happened to a text only after it was written. Decisions about reviewing could have been made by scores of different people on opposite sides of the Atlantic, guided by different standards of poetic quality, and often by factors entirely unrelated to the text—politics, notoriety, marketing. So this is not a situation where we know that there is a pattern in a group of texts and set out to test an algorithm's ability to capture the pattern. Rather, we are testing whether the social phenomenon of poetic prominence has any textual correlate at all. The answer could have been no. But it turns out that poetic prominence does correlate with a particular kind of writing. Further, that "kind of writing" can be modeled simply by counting words, and it remained rather stable between 1820 and 1919.

Since works by prominent writers seem too diverse to produce this kind of stable boundary, we suspected at first that the source of stability must be located in our random sample. The volumes of poetry we don't usually read must be united by some obvious feature: Maybe they're all religious? Or just blatantly awful? One way to test this hypothesis was to ask whether human beings would find it equally easy to identify the provenance of texts.

So we presented pages from both samples to graduate students and professors who study nineteenth- or early-twentieth-century literature and asked them to guess whether each page had been selected from reviewed volumes or randomly sampled from a library. We told them when each volume had been published and let them know whether each guess was right or wrong as they went along. Trained readers were right 64% of the time. It is not an apples-to-apples comparison with the model (which got to read whole books, not single pages), but it does reveal at least that there is no difference between the samples screamingly obvious to human readers. In fact, I suspect human readers achieved 64% accuracy more by recognizing particular famous passages than by framing general theories about poetic prestige.

So how is a statistical model able to predict poetic reception so reliably? That's a good question. But before exploring it, it may be useful to compare a similar model trained on reviewed and random fiction. Here (figure 3.2), predicting reception is significantly more difficult; a model trained on evidence from 1850 to 1949 is right only 72.5% of the time. The pattern is otherwise very similar, down to a very slight upward drift in the model showing that works of fiction generally move (slowly) in the direction of prominent examples.

Since the model of fiction is not quite as good as our model of poetry, we might be tempted to speculate that poetic prestige is inherently easier to capture for some deep formal reason. Perhaps word choice is just more central to poetic quality? Perhaps. But before going too far down that path, it is important to notice

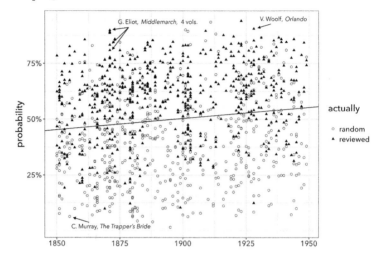

FIGURE 3.2. Probability of belonging to reviewed fiction set. A model of prestige in American and British fiction, 1850–1949, achieving 72.5% accuracy. The trend line is a linear regression on the points plotted.

that the strength of the model depends not just on the difference between poetry and fiction but on the way these texts are selected. Our samples of poetry and fiction come mostly from magazines, like the *Atlantic* or *Fortnightly Review*, that addressed a broad educated audience. But there are also a range of avant-garde little magazines in the mix, and when we compose a sample of ninety-five fiction volumes selected only from reviews in these little magazines, we get a clearer boundary between the reviewed and random samples: 83% accuracy. So it is not by any means impossible for the prestige of fiction to be signaled clearly by word choice; it just doesn't happen to be true yet for the bulk of the fiction in our 1850–1949 sample.

This is an important test for the experiment we are running, analogous to a dose-response relationship in clinical trials. If a drug is really curing or causing a disease, then one would expect some relationship between a patient's health and the amount of the drug he or she took. Similarly, if our model is really measuring social stratification, then an even more narrowly defined group of texts, sampled from consciously selective venues, ought to be even easier to model—and it is. We still have to proceed carefully when interpreting these results. Two groups of texts can differ in many ways at once, so it isn't safe to assume that our model is capturing literary prestige and nothing but prestige. Prestige is almost certainly mixed here with other issues: for instance, subgenres that happen to be more (or less) common in the reviewed set. This makes subtle differences in accuracy difficult to interpret. But it seems at least plausible that fiction is harder than poetry to model because of the historical factor this experiment was designed to measure. Fiction may just have been less strongly sorted by prestige than poetry—at least until one gets into the little magazines of the twentieth century.

The Secrets of Literary Distinction

So how is a statistical model able to predict which volumes of poetry or fiction will be reviewed? And what *was* the secret to getting reviewed in this period? I will only be able to provide a rough answer. The models described above use thousands of variables (which are simply thousands of common words in the texts). Models of this kind are not magic tricks. Things built by human beings can be taken apart by human beings: it is simple enough to identify the words that make a difference in the models. But *thousands* of words make a difference, because literary prestige is related to many intersecting themes. The interpretive problem we confront here lies not in machine learning but in the actual complexity of literary reception—which is not required to map onto a single thesis that can be crisply explained in five pages.

Because the models produced by machine learning are complex, they can faithfully and rigorously measure the actual strength of the boundary between two groups of texts. But because these models are nearly as complex as the actual social boundaries at issue, they also leave a lot of explanatory work to the interpreter. A list of the twenty top words in a model is not guaranteed to be revealing. Scanning through the whole list of twenty-six hundred words (in the case of the poetry model) is more illuminating. But I can hardly ask readers to do that with me—and in any case, the significance of a word is sometimes only clear when we see it in context. I have found that the clearest and liveliest way to explicate a model is to read a few passages over its shoulder.

So let's consider how our model of poetic prestige might respond to a couple of exemplary passages. To make this clearer, I have divided the model's twenty-six hundred variables into three groups: the top nine hundred words, which markedly increase a poem's perceived likelihood of being reviewed, are represented in boldface. The bottom nine hundred, which markedly decrease that likelihood, are italicized. All others are typeset normally (this includes words too rare to be included in the model, as well as the middle eight hundred words—which don't individually have a huge effect). We'll start with the conclusion of Christina Rossetti's "Echo" (1865), which the model sees as very likely to be reviewed:

> Yet come to **me** in **dreams**, that I may *live*
>   My *very* **life** *again* tho' **cold** in **death**:
> Come **back** to **me** in **dreams**, that I may give
>   Pulse for pulse, **breath** for **breath**:
>   Speak low, lean low,
>   As **long** *ago*, my love, **how long** *ago*.[9]

One can detect traces of the advice that writing teachers still give: "use definite, specific, concrete language."[10] The model loves "breath for breath" and being cold in death. By contrast, it is a bit dubious about "*live* / My *very* **life** *again*." If it were actually judging poems, the model might be wrong to cavil there: the tautological abstraction provides contrast to the rest of the language in this stanza and is appropriate for a speaker struggling to

---

9. Christina Rossetti, "Echo," in *Goblin Market and Other Poems*, 2nd ed. (London: Macmillan, 1865), 81.

10. William Strunk and E. B. White, *The Elements of Style* (1959; New York: Penguin, 2007), 37.

express the immensity of loss. But of course the model can't make that kind of contextual judgment; it just generally recommends concrete language.

Even on that point, however, the model is not quite consistent. It likes certain abstractions too, such as *dreams* and *death*—although, perversely enough, not *live*. It likes *cold*, but not *hot*; *fear*, but not *joy*; *bitter*, but not *sweet*. In fact, we may as well admit that this model is happiest when poems are a bit desolate. *Brooding, blind, hollow*, and *harsh* are some of its favorite words. It has an allergy to things that are *kind* or *noble*. It doesn't even like *homes*. We can see why if we look at the volumes at the very bottom of its list—the ones it is rightly confident will never be reviewed. Many of these have some inspirational or hortatory purpose; they are about equally divided between religious and political topics but share a reliance on positive emblems of collective emotion. In *Memorial or Decoration Day* (1891), for instance, George Loomis invokes "those who battled for these *homes* of *ours*, / And *precious* blood on *Freedom's* altar *shed*."[11] By no means all the volumes in the random set are this sentimental, but there are enough (thoroughly obscure) examples of this style to make the model wary not only of positive abstractions but of the first-person plural in general.

I hope the contrast between the diction of Loomis and Rossetti is vivid—but it is vivid, of course, because I spent hours combing through poems to find passages that economically illustrated the contrast I felt was central here. To interpret this boundary in a way less dependent on cherry-picking, we might ask how the model's predictions line up with semantic lists extracted from the Harvard General Inquirer.

Let me emphasize that I am not presenting table 3.2 as a complete or objective account of the model. A list of the top five correlations leaves out many subtler patterns (feminine pronouns, for instance, are also more prominent in the reviewed sample).

11. George Loomis, *Memorial or Decoration Day: A Poem Founded on Facts* (n.p.: n.p., 1891), http://catalog.hathitrust.org/Record/009558911.

TABLE 3.2. Categories that distinguish reviewed and random volumes of poetry. The frequencies of 118 semantic categories from the Harvard General Inquirer were calculated for the 720 volumes plotted in figure 3.1. Then the categories were sorted by correlation with the volumes' predicted probabilities of coming from the reviewed set.

Correlate with reviewed poetry	r	Correlate with random poetry	r
Colors	.398	Positive sentiment	.530
Body parts	.281	Virtue	.526
First-person singular	.233	Power	.425
Natural objects	.228	Dependence or obligation	.379
Weakness	.194	Political terms	.362

Moreover, I am certain that literary scholars would blink in puzzlement at many specific choices in the General Inquirer's lists of words. (*Astray, asleep, baby,* and *cease,* for instance, all connote "weakness" in this system!) I am invoking the General Inquirer here not as an objective authority but merely as a second witness—something that can provide a check on my own cherry-picking impulses (and my preference for Christina Rossetti).

But the issues at stake in poetic prestige are so clear that these caveats may seem unnecessary. Whether we close-read passages or use the General Inquirer's categories, it is easy to see that the obscure poets in our random sample lean toward abstraction and positive sentiment, whereas reviewed poets emphasize physical description—especially of colors, nature, and the human body. On the other side of the model, if we unpack the Inquirer's terms "power" and "dependence," we find that randomly sampled volumes emphasize words associated with social relations. The reviewed writers, by contrast, use more first-person singular pronouns. All of this boils down to a fairly clear contrast between embodied lyric subjectivity and an older mode of poetic authority that is more didactic, sentimental, and collective. We may imagine that the struggle between these modes was resolved once and for all in Romanticism, but in reality the older mode persisted, and elite poetic culture continued to be defined by an ever fiercer rejection of it, all the way through the early twentieth century.

A model of prestige in fiction is harder to describe. To begin with, you may notice that the correlation coefficients in table 3.3

TABLE 3.3. Categories that distinguish reviewed and random volumes of fiction. The frequencies of 118 semantic categories from the Harvard General Inquirer were calculated for the twelve hundred volumes plotted in figure 3.2. Then the categories were sorted by correlation with the volumes' predicted probabilities of coming from the reviewed set.

Correlate with reviewed fiction	r	Correlate with random fiction	r
Knowledge and awareness	.294	Active (rather than passive) orientation	.447
Natural processes	.195	Social relations	.418
Natural objects	.191	Travel	.394
Understatement and qualification	.175	Dependence and obligation	.347
Comparison	.170	Achievement	.334

are slightly lower than those in table 3.2. The patterns are less crisp than they were in poetry. Reviewed fiction, in particular, is hard to characterize semantically. Here, as with poetry, the correlation coefficients suggest that it may be easier to describe books that didn't get reviewed in elite venues.

A few of these patterns will be familiar: natural objects on the reviewed side, for instance, and social relations or obligations on the random side. The textual signs of prestige in fiction are not altogether different from the signs of prestige in poetry. In fact if one compares the predictions of the two models, run on a superset of all the volumes in this experiment (fiction and poetry mixed together), they correlate positively and have 13.5% of their variance in common ($r = .367$)—which suggests that the criteria of distinction in poetry and fiction overlap in a medium-sized area that might simply be labeled "literary distinction." One important rule governing literary distinction from 1850 through 1919, where the models overlap, was apparently to emphasize sensory description of natural objects rather than a direct account of power in the social world. The emergent definition of literary language we saw in chapter 1—expressing literariness above all as sensory immediacy—was presumably fostered and rewarded by this definition of prestige.

But interpretation of this kind needs to proceed cautiously. The area of overlap between the models of poetry and fiction is a relatively clear spot in an otherwise muddled picture. If we look further into the fiction model, internal contradictions emerge.

The criteria of fictional prestige in table 3.3 include concrete objects, to be sure, but also words used to qualify an assertion and abstractions that imply awareness. And the concepts that characterize the random set include not just social abstractions but words associated with physical travel. If we think about the way these themes play out in fiction, it may be possible to resolve some of the apparent contradictions. I suspect the vulgarity of travel, for instance, reflects the prominence of adventure fiction in the random sample (ranging from Mayne Reid to Zane Grey).

But there are also aspects of this model that resist thematic summary. To understand these we may need to think judgmentally about a boundary between cliché and precision. For instance, consider this passage from *The Trapper's Bride; or, Spirit of Adventure* (1855), by Charles Augustus Murray. Our hero (also named Charles) is about to be rushed by a bear. Once again I am italicizing words that significantly reduce the chance of review (in this case the bottom eight hundred) and boldfacing words that significantly increase it (the top eight hundred), leaving four hundred in the middle unmarked.

> *Quick* as lightning these *thoughts* and wishes *flashed* through his mind. **Seeing** his peril, in an *instant* he had seized his rifle by the barrel, and raising it by the *side* of his head, prepared to deal his foe a tremendous blow. But bruin was **too** good a boxer. . . . The next *instant*, Charles felt the **strong legs** of the shaggy beast **folded** about him, and **pressing** him in a *closer* and *closer* hug. He *dropped* his rifle from his hand, and struggled to **draw** his *knife*.[12]

On the whole, this book is a third-rate version of the Leatherstocking Tales. Savages are noble; love happens at first sight; our model of prestige locates it near the very bottom of the list. Even physical struggle is described in a hackneyed way, and readers may notice that the model of prestige zeroes in on a particularly painful aspect of this description—a conventional rhetoric of breathlessness. Thoughts have to flash "quick as lightning," and

---

12. Charles Augustus Murray, *The Trapper's Bride; or, Spirit of Adventure* (Louisville: C. Hagan, 1855), 124.

each instantaneous event has to be accompanied by an explicit reminder that it took a mere "instant."

Obviously there is nothing inherently bad about *instant* or *flashed*; these words have many legitimate uses. Our model has only learned to hate them because they are overused in obscure works of fiction. But "liable to be used in clichés" is not part of a word's semantic definition. A resource like the General Inquirer is necessarily going to struggle to characterize the common element that links *instant* to other words the model hates, like *desperate, breathed,* and *hearts.*[13] So a reader hoping to understand the model in detail may have to do some close reading of specific passages in order to recognize the patterns that make these words symptomatic. I have done that for both poetry and fiction, but I think close reading is especially necessary for the fiction model: it is possible to generalize about the qualities that undermine prestige in poetry, but the prestige of fiction can be diluted by a hundred different forms of laziness.

The same thing applies in reverse to highly regarded fiction, although the qualities that earn it high regard may be even harder to define. Semantically, there is nothing notable about the bold-faced words in this passage from *Middlemarch*:

> Many who knew her thought it a **pity** that so substantive and rare a **creature** should have been absorbed into the life of **another**, and be only *known* in a **certain circle** as wife and mother. But no one stated what **else** that was in her power she **ought** rather to have done.[14]

Somehow the model detects a quality here that is likely to achieve prominence. To understand how it can do so, we might reflect on the habits of thought that produced these words in this particular passage. "A certain circle," for instance, has paused to acknowledge a limitation on its own social description, while "else" and "ought" are used in counterfactual moral reasoning. The language

---

13. For one solution, see Andreas van Cranenburgh, "Cliché Expressions in Literary and Genre Novels," *Proceedings of the Workshop on Computational Linguistics for Cultural Heritage, Social Sciences, Humanities, and Literature* (2018).

14. George Eliot, *Middlemarch* (Edinburgh: W. Blackwood, 1871–72), 4:366.

is not recondite, but it may be the sort of language that was used by careful thinkers in the nineteenth century. And yet, of course, all the model really knows is that these words tend to be used by other authors reviewed in prominent venues.

I have suggested that we may need to project a bit, and think judgmentally, in order to understand how a model like this works. But we don't necessarily need to endorse the model's implied judgments. Standards change; these are just a set of standards that happened to govern the reviewing of fiction in certain venues between 1850 and 1949. On the other hand, I would admit that this conventional relativist proviso rings a little hollower than usual given the remarkable stability we actually see in figures 3.1 and 3.2. Although aesthetic judgments change, they seem to change very slowly, at a pace that might be difficult to distinguish from permanence using our ordinary critical tool kit. This sort of tectonic drift is a matter of considerable importance for the humanities: the significance of our subject is deeply bound up with forms of cultural value that are historically contingent but in practice very durable. To say "contingent" and "durable" at once may seem like a contradiction. But one advantage of numbers, paradoxically enough, is that they allow us to be patient with this ambiguity: they can characterize literary value as durable without affirming it as universal.

How Quickly Does Reception Change?

A central argument of this book is that many important forms of cultural change play out more slowly, over longer timelines, than our generation-scaled narratives have been comfortable acknowledging. But I want to carefully distinguish that observation from a sweeping claim that cultural change, in general, is slow. As I stressed at the beginning of this chapter, there are always multiple directions of change at different scales of description. A new book or restaurant may make a big splash in a particular year; that's an important, sudden change. At the same time, it can be true that cuisine has been drifting slowly along a different vector for a century. I'm claiming that phenomena of the latter kind have been hard for us to describe and are more important than we have so far understood. I'm not suggesting that they are the only kind of change that ever happens.

In fact, I don't want to claim to have measured the pace of literary change *in general* at all. To measure change, one has to define features that matter, and I doubt that readers will ever reach consensus on a single set of features that matter for all possible literary questions. I have relied heavily on word counts in this book because words can be weighted to flexibly capture many specific axes of differentiation. But that doesn't mean that a list of common words, weighted equally, would be a universally applicable metric for all forms of change. It remains an open question whether a metric of that kind even exists.

Measuring change in reception is a more tractable problem because it involves a specified boundary between groups of texts. If our models predict that boundary reliably, we know that they have captured something important about reception; if one model can predict the boundary reasonably well across a century, we know that some important aspects of reception changed slowly. Literature itself may have changed in other ways: D. H. Lawrence writes things about the sex lives of whales that would have made Tennyson blush. For some readers, that may be an important difference. But it will do little to alter a model of reception unless there was a point between 1820 and 1919 when erotic empathy with whales started to make the difference between poetic success and obscurity. In practice, the textual differences associated with success seem to have changed slowly.

To be confident on this point, I have compared multiple models. The model represented above tries to find a pattern that can explain a whole century at once. It is significant that it succeeds, but that isn't what we ordinarily mean by evidence of historical continuity, because the modeling process is actively trying to find an explanation that will cover this whole period. A more intuitive way to assess change is to train models on different segments of the timeline and then compare them. For instance, we could train a model only on volumes from one quarter century but ask it to make predictions about the rest of the century.

That actually works. Models trained on a quarter century of fiction are right (on average) about 71% of the volumes in the whole century; they lose only 1.5% accuracy compared to a model trained on everything. Models trained on a quarter century of poetry are right about 75.9% of the volumes in the poetry data set—a bigger loss (of 4%), since models of poetic prestige were more accurate to begin with. But accuracy is still durable enough to suggest that the standards that persist for twenty-five years will remain largely the same for the rest of the century. This gives us a rough and ready answer to the question posed in this section: How quickly does reception change? At the boundary we model here (getting reviewed in selective periodicals), the standards we can model at all seem to have changed rather slowly.

There are many caveats to consider here, the main one being "the standards we can model at all." Many aspects of prestige are not captured in our models because they involve social connections or marketing or the idiosyncratic standards of a single magazine—or concepts that are simply hard to capture. Since these factors escape our model altogether, we have no way to measure their rate of change. It seems plausible that the idiosyncratic personal factors involved in prestige, for instance, would be quite volatile. But even if that is true, it remains interesting, I think, that the part of prestige overtly legible in the literary text changes so slowly.

The method I have outlined above could also be used to pose a number of more complex and ambitious questions. For instance, standards of distinction seem to change more rapidly in poetry than in fiction—in the sense that poetic models lose more accuracy (4%) when they are restricted to a quarter century of evidence. But I don't have confidence in the statistical significance of that observation. To know whether poetic reception actually changes more rapidly, I would have to compare many random samples, to find out whether this difference between fiction and poetry is durable. I haven't answered that question yet, but it would repay more research: if opinions about poetry are really more volatile than opinions about fiction, that's something literary historians should know. We might also use the method of mutual recognition developed in chapter 2 to ask how the pace of change has varied across the timeline. The evidence before us already strongly suggests that we won't find the radical reversals that historians sometimes like to posit. But we might find subtler fluctuations in the pace of change, and those could still be important.

Synchronic Prestige and Diachronic Change

Although I have characterized reviewing patterns as mostly stable from 1820 to 1950, there were of course many changes, some of which are visible in the figures above. In all these models, the mean probability that a volume will be reviewed appears to increase across time. That is not literally true. Reviewed and random volumes are evenly distributed across the timeline, so the probability of review remains constant. But the words common in reviewed volumes (across the whole timeline) also tend to become more common in *all* volumes as we approach the end of the timeline, so the cloud of data points always tilts up. The "bar" that volumes have to clear in order to be reviewed, in other words, seems to slide upward.

This pattern is durable. It appears in both poetry and fiction, although it is more dramatic in poetry. If we divide a century of literary evidence into two parts and train models on each, we see an upward slope within each part. Nothing about the modeling process itself compels this upward slope. We don't see a strong, consistent tilt if we predict other social boundaries, like genre or authorial gender. In short, it seems likely that we are looking at evidence of a general relationship between literary prestige and historical change. Diachronic change across a period recapitulates the period's synchronic axis of distinction.

A conjecture this broad needs a few provisos. We don't yet know with certainty that this will happen outside the period

1820–1949; we're just hypothesizing that it will. Although the pattern is definitely significant ($p < .0001$), the rate of change is not huge: the bar for poetry slides up about 2% per decade, for fiction about 1%. This drift relative to synchronic standards is interestingly durable, but it isn't the only kind of change that can happen in literary history: many different changes are always happening, and many of them won't be captured by a model of prestige. Later in this chapter, for instance, I'll discuss evidence about sales. The boundary between best sellers and other books can be used to train a model just as we have used the decisions made by reviewers. When I do that, I again see an upward drift across time in the direction of the features that correlate with sales, although this trend is interestingly not quite as clear or consistent as the pattern generated by models of prestige.

In short, I am not proposing a monocausal explanation for literary change. Literature moves in a direction shaped by many factors at once. What we see in any individual model is a projection of the actual, multidimensional vector of change onto a simpler, one-dimensional axis of measurement; it is, so to speak, one component of the vector. The interaction between different components, and different social pressures, is an obvious subject for further research. Moreover, even in the models we have defined, the arc of change can bend. A model of a whole century looks like a single line segment, but if separate decade-long models could be plotted in a high-dimensional space, they might trace a curved trajectory. So it is not as though the whole sweep of literary history has to move in any single direction forever. I am just suggesting that whenever scholars do define an axis of social distinction in a given period, they will see upward motion in the period itself relative to the axis they have defined. This pattern isn't shocking. It is easy to imagine reasons why it might happen. But that is not to say that we expected it or already understand why it does happen.

It is actually a little odd that a model trained on the 1860s sees works from the 1870s as more likely to be reviewed than the works it was trained on. I don't want to claim that I understand yet why this happens. We might speculate, for instance, that standards tend to drift upward because critics and authors respond directly to pressure from reviewers or because they imitate, and slightly exaggerate, the standards already implicit in prominent examples. In that case, synchronic standards would produce diachronic change. But causality could also work the other way: a long-term pattern of diachronic change could itself create synchronic standards, if readers in each decade along the way formed their criteria of literary distinction partly by contrasting the latest thing to the embarrassing past. In fact, causal arrows could run in both of these directions.

There are ways to untangle this causal knot. It is interesting, for instance, that predicted probabilities of review correlate with authors' dates of birth more strongly than they correlate with publication dates. This detail suggests that the causal processes responsible for change are located fairly early in an author's life, and it may hint that authors imitate prestigious examples. But as social scientists understand all too well, causal processes are hard to trace in detail. Untangling the knot is worth attempting, but it could easily require a whole separate book. Nor do we actually need a causal explanation of this phenomenon to see that it could have far-reaching consequences for literary history. The model I have presented already suggests that some things scholars tend to describe as rejections of tradition—modernist insistence on the concrete image, for instance—are better explained as continuations of a long-term trend, guided by established standards.

Gender and Nationality

The method used in this chapter has a significant weak spot, which is that it relies on contrasting two groups of texts that are expected to be generally alike, except for one difference—their probability of being reviewed in elite periodicals. The problem is that there are always multiple differences between groups of texts. If the reviewed sample also contained more British men, for instance, our model of prestige might become in part a model of

British masculinity. The model isn't explicitly told about authors' genders, and I have normalized spelling to avoid spurious contrasts between *honour* and *honor*, but nationality and gender are still dimly legible in an author's diction. So even when a model knows only about the language of the work, it is possible that predictions about reception could seem accurate only because they were tacitly based on the depressingly reliable assumption that works by Americans, or women, wouldn't get reviewed.

Problems of this kind are becoming important in twenty-first-century life, where they are often diagnosed as "algorithmic bias." Economic and racial categories may intersect, for instance, but people shouldn't have their loan applications declined because they belong to a racial minority. In historical inquiry, the same problem emerges, but *bias* may not be exactly the right word to apply in this context. At any rate, historians are interested in the intersection of social preferences; it is not an aspect of the past that we simply factor out. It is quite possible, for instance, that Britishness really was a significant component of literary prestige in nineteenth-century America. A model of literary culture that covered its eyes to avoid seeing that preference wouldn't represent the period.

On the other hand, historians do want to know when one social category defines another. For instance, if a model of prestige turned out to be mostly reducible to Britishness, plus masculinity, that's something we would want to acknowledge. So without forcing our sample of the past to be unrealistically balanced, we would like to have some way to measure the effects of imbalances. Fortunately, quantitative methods make it easy to look at the same evidence from several different angles and measure the interactions between social categories. We can never be sure that we have checked all possible factors, but large variables that slice right through the middle of the literary field (like gender and nationality) can definitely be checked.

In our data set, women are underrepresented, contributing only 38% of the volumes in fiction and 25% in poetry. Just as importantly, they are distributed a little unequally across the reviewed and random samples—slightly more likely than men to be reviewed in poetry and significantly less so in fiction. This imbalance raises the possibility that our models of "prestige" might be leaning on gender as a clue. To measure the size of the effect, we can construct alternate models of prestige where men and women are represented equally and distributed equally across the reviewed and random samples (as well as across time). But when I train these balanced models, I get a picture of prestige that is not in practice very different. Accuracy declines less than 2% in fiction and doesn't decline at all in poetry. Moreover, balanced models make predictions that are very similar to the original version; they have 84% of their variance in common. This is not to deny that women writers confronted barriers and were judged unequally; their sheer underrepresentation in the data set, by itself, is an eloquent fact. But the criteria of prestige that we can model using textual evidence don't seem mostly reducible to gender.

The question of nationality is more vexed, both because the Britishness of British literature may have been an overt source of prestige and because our samples are affected differently by the Atlantic Ocean. The reviewed samples used in this chapter were drawn from both American and British periodicals. But the "random" samples were drawn from HathiTrust Digital Library, which mainly aggregates the collections of American libraries. These libraries contain plenty of British books, but they do tend to contain more obscure volumes from San Francisco or Cincinnati than from (say) Leeds. As a result, the random sample, especially in poetry, tends to favor Americans. Either for this library-specific reason or because British poets were genuinely more prominent, nationality becomes a significant confounding factor in the poetry model. When the poetry data set is rebalanced to represent British and American authors equally, the model drops to 71.8% accuracy and makes predictions that are significantly changed (having only 69.5% of their variance in common with the original model). The effects on fiction are not equally dramatic; in fact, there is no loss of accuracy at all in fiction when the model is balanced across the Atlantic. So, in short, the prestige of British poetry is the only case I can find where authorial demographics clearly distort our model of prestige. Rather than being a mere sampling error, I suspect this represents a real association between nationality and poetic capital. But more research would be needed to say for sure.

Separating the Axes of Popularity and Prestige

The original goal of this experiment was to test whether reviewed and random samples would become easier to differentiate as time passed. Critical tradition suggested that distinctions between popular and elite literary culture grew sharper somewhere in this period—either because a "great divide" emerged suddenly at the beginning of the twentieth century or because reading audiences specialized slowly "over the course of the nineteenth century, as the increasingly centralized media and entertainment industries interacted with the growth of education."[15] It seemed reasonable to hypothesize that serious literary writing would develop its own idiom, diverging from the quicker patter of (say) detective and adventure fiction. If so, models of prestige should get more accurate over time, as it became easier to distinguish high literary culture from the rest of the literary field.

The pattern I actually found was subtler and more complex. Literary culture does diversify across this century, but not in a way well captured by a story about sharpening distinctions and widening divides. Those metaphors are too one-dimensional to capture a change that actually involved several different axes of distinction. Instead of imagining that literature became more strongly sorted along a single axis (separating elite literary taste from mass culture) we should imagine two largely parallel axes of distinction that slowly unfold to become perpendicular.

15. Janet Gray, "Popular Poetry," in *Encyclopedia of American Poetry: The Nineteenth Century*, ed. Eric Haralson (New York: Routledge, 2001), 347.

The one-dimensional approach I began with was not totally fruitless. If I peer very carefully at the accuracy of models in different periods, I can point to a few pieces of evidence that suggest literature was growing more strongly sorted by prestige. If one divides the model of poetic prestige into four quarter-century models, for instance, one finds that accuracy before 1845 is only 66.3%. After 1845, it stays consistently above 80%. So something appears to change (either in poetry itself or in reviewing practices) around the middle of the nineteenth century. In fiction we can see a similar change at the other end of the timeline. A model restricted to works reviewed in twentieth-century little magazines is significantly more accurate than a model based on general-circulation magazines in the nineteenth century. But if these isolated signs of stronger differentiation feel like cherry-picked examples, you are not wrong! Neither poetry nor fiction really displays what I had expected to see: a sustained trend in the middle of the timeline, indicating a general hardening of boundaries between elite literary taste and everything else.

But once I describe my hypothesis that way, it may be easy to see my mistake. "Elite literary taste" and "everything else" cover a lot of ground. Within the reviewed sample of fiction, it turned out that it mattered deeply whether we found a review in general intellectual journalism or in a little magazine. And within the random sample, I discovered an even deeper divide between works that were left out of serious reviewing because they seemed too sensational or popular and works left out because they were merely obscure. I may not have fully appreciated this difference at the beginning of the experiment. But one learns a lot, informally, while sampling hundreds of books from the depths of a library.

So I decided to take a second crack at the problem, adding another axis of analysis in order to tease out some of the complexities obscured by a one-dimensional model. To my existing model of prestige in fiction, I added information about sales. Here I was following the lead of Pierre Bourdieu, who famously mapped nineteenth-century French literature using economic capital and cultural capital as two perpendicular axes.[16] When I am trying to understand the slow differentiation of literary and nonliterary language, Bourdieu's theories about the emergence of an autonomous cultural field have often been a useful source of hunches. But instead of simply postulating economic and cultural capital as distinct forces in the nineteenth century, I could proceed empirically in order to test the real relation between them. (To be clear, this is what Bourdieu himself often did when writing about contemporary culture. Perspectival modeling allows us to pose the same questions about a century where people are no longer able to reply to surveys.)

In designing this experiment, I was aware that researchers at the Stanford Literary Lab had also developed a quantitative version of Bourdieu's map, using academic citations as a proxy for "cultural capital" and the number of editions in libraries as a proxy for "economic success."[17] The Stanford model was appealing, but since nineteenth-century novels were not taught in nineteenth-century classrooms, academic citations could provide only a belated measure of cultural capital. Reviews are not a perfect measure either, but I hoped that replacing academic citations with contemporary reviews would create a model closer to the shape of the literary field at the time of publication.

I also needed a way to model sales. Ideally, one would simply look up the sales figures for each of the roughly two thousand volumes in this data set. But that's not possible. Detailed sales records haven't always been preserved, and they certainly aren't organized by any central index. On the other hand, best-seller lists are relatively easy to find. From 1895 forward, a series of different periodicals reported the top ten or fifteen bestselling works of fiction in each year. Before 1895, evidence is less reliable, but a number of book historians have constructed lists of American or British best sellers based on some mixture of hard evidence

16. Pierre Bourdieu, "The Field of Cultural Production, or: The Economic World Reversed," in *The Field of Cultural Production: Essays on Art and Literature*, ed. Randal Johnson (New York: Columbia University Press, 1993), 29–73.

17. Algee-Hewitt et al., "Canon/Archive."

and personal impressions.[18] These lists tell us, of course, relatively little about an individual book. Either it appeared on a list of best sellers or it didn't. But if we back out to discuss authors, we can construct a more flexible metric by asking how many times an author appeared on any of these lists. Prolific authors who sold widely on both sides of the Atlantic will appear many times; those who succeeded more rarely or more locally will only appear once or twice. Most authors, of course, won't appear at all.

This is the remaining problem with our strategy: it leaves a huge gulf between authors who produced one best seller and the vast majority who sold reasonably well but never quite made it into the year's top fifteen books. To fill that gap we can rely on the measure of popularity the Stanford team used—the number of editions published roughly in the author's lifetime and pre-served in libraries. This isn't exactly the same kind of economic success measured by best-seller lists (since libraries' purchasing patterns differ from ordinary readers'), but the two measures cor-relate closely enough that we can fuse them to produce a com-promise estimate, relying more heavily on best-seller lists for authors who appear on them and more heavily on a count of editions for authors who don't. Moreover, we don't have to invent this compromise arbitrarily: a method called "empirical Bayes" gives us a principled way to quantify uncertainty, so our estimate can be more confident where lots of evidence is available and more cautious where it isn't. We end up with an estimate of how often each author would have appeared on a best-seller list if it were possible to appear fractional times.

Armed with these estimates, we can proceed to make broad comparisons between the market prominence of authors in the

18. Altick, *English Common Reader*; Clive Bloom, *Bestsellers: Popular Fiction since 1900* (Houndmills: Palgrave Macmillan, 2008); Alice Payne Hackett and James Henry Burke, *80 Years of Best Sellers, 1895–1975* (New York: R. R. Bowker, 1977); Q. D. Leavis, *Fiction and the Reading Public* (London: Chatto and Windus, 1935); Frank Luther Mott, *Golden Multitudes: The Story of Best Sellers in the United States* (New York: R. R. Bowker, 1947); John Unsworth, 20th Century American Bestsellers, accessed June 1, 2017, http://bestsellers.lib.virginia.edu.

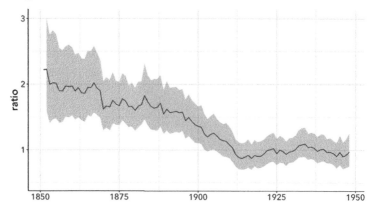

FIGURE 3.3. Ratio of best sellers by reviewed authors to those by random authors. Estimated appearances on best-seller lists for the average author of reviewed fiction are compared to appearances for the average author in the random dataset. The ratio between the two is plotted as a twenty-year moving average, surrounded by a 90% confidence band.

reviewed and random samples, as shown in figure 3.3. In the middle of the nineteenth century, reviewed authors are roughly twice as likely to appear on a list of best sellers. Most of the period's highly regarded writers (like George Eliot or Nathaniel Hawthorne) also sold plenty of books. But as we move forward through time, there are more and more best sellers in the random sample; by the 1920s, the ratio is roughly even.

This shift, I think, is what unsettled contemporary observers. It was increasingly possible to have economic success without the critical success that had previously seemed its inseparable accompaniment. Confident separation of these two modes of distinction is what makes Jasper Milvain's cynicism in George Gissing's *New Grub Street* (1891) so shocking: "Never in my life shall I do anything of solid literary value; I shall always despise the people I write for. But my path will be that of success." Milvain doesn't deny that it may be possible to combine money and critical acclaim. He merely points out that there is an easier path open for "the literary man of 1882." "Oh, if you can be a George Eliot, begin at the earliest opportunity. I merely suggested what seemed practicable."[19] We have inherited a later, darker version of this story, where popular success and highbrow appreciation are described as becoming actually incompatible. Writers must "choose between these alternatives," as Q. D. Leavis put it in *Fiction and the Reading Public*.[20] I originally tried to find a divide between elite and mass culture because my expectations had been shaped by that gloomy account of a hardening dichotomy. But up to 1949, at any rate, Jasper Milvain's insouciance is a better account of what actually happened. Literary prestige and market success did not become incompatible, but they did lose their tight correlation.

To get a more particularized sense of what that "loss of correlation" means, we can glance at two pictures of the literary field separated by fifty years. Now that we have estimates of cultural prestige and of market success, it is possible to empirically reproduce the social map of literature that Bourdieu offered as a regulative theory. Each of the bubbles (or triangles) in figure 3.4 represents an author of fiction. The horizontal axis estimates authors' relative sales; the vertical axis estimates prestige, measured as a probability of being reviewed in elite publications. In both cases, the estimates are very rough; no inferences should be drawn from the fact that one author is positioned just slightly above another. But the overall shape of the literary field is interesting.

In the middle of the nineteenth century, authors are loosely organized in an oval with a clear upward slope. I have plotted the slope of the trend as a dashed line, but more important is the correlation coefficient ($r = .26$), which describes the strength of the trend relative to other variation. As sales increase, so does critical prestige. There are only a few exceptions. In the lower right

19. George Gissing, *New Grub Street*, ed. John Goode (Oxford: Oxford University Press, 1993), 74, 8, 13.

20. Leavis, *Fiction and the Reading Public*, 263.

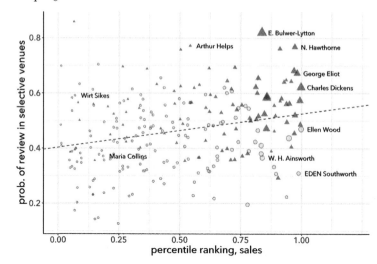

FIGURE 3.4. The literary field, 1850–74. Cultural prominence (measured as probability of review in selective journals) and economic success (estimated percentile ranking of the author's sales in his or her lifetime), British and American fiction, 1850–74. Authors are sized to reflect the number of volumes in HathiTrust; triangles were found reviewed in elite periodicals.

corner of the map, it is possible to find a few high-selling authors who are predicted to lack prestige—notably, for instance, the popular American novelist E. D. E. N. Southworth. It is harder to find outliers in the upper left corner—authors with critical prestige but no sales. Arthur Helps, a Cambridge apostle, is a fairly lonely figure.

Fast-forward fifty years, to figure 3.5, and we see a different picture. The ascending slope of this cloud is now harder to see; mathematically, there is still a faint correlation between prestige and sales ($r = .13$), but it is so faint that the overall picture now looks square. The upper left corner of the graph is now populated with authors who would eventually come to dominate syllabi (James Joyce, Gertrude Stein, Zora Neale Hurston). The lower right corner is also more richly fleshed out, with a number of writers in the front rank of sales although the language of their works isn't the sort usually esteemed by critics. In fact, if

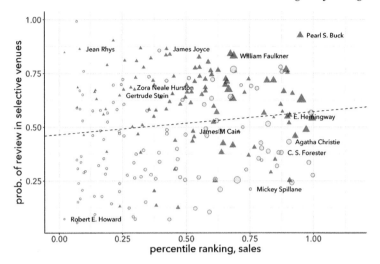

FIGURE 3.5. The literary field, 1925–49. Cultural prominence (measured as probability of review in selective journals) and economic success (estimated percentile ranking of the author's sales in his or her lifetime), British and American fiction, 1925–49. Authors are sized to reflect the number of volumes in HathiTrust; triangles were found reviewed in elite periodicals.

one focuses only on well-known names—slanting down from James Joyce to Mickey Spillane—it is possible to see how contemporaries might have gotten the impression that sales correlate negatively with critical prestige. That isn't actually true about the bigger picture, as the people in the lower left corner of the field would sadly remind us. But an observer who focused on the right side of the map might perhaps perceive a negative correlation. The real change is better described as diversification. Where the mid-nineteenth-century map could almost reduce into a single axis (prominence versus obscurity), the mid-twentieth-century map really has to be characterized using two separate dimensions.

Distant readers are sometimes accused of laboriously proving things that other critics already suspected. I have resisted that argument fiercely when I think it is hindsight bias. But in this section of the book, I would acknowledge it is largely true. Many observers—all the way back to George Gissing—have implied that commercial success and literary judgment somehow parted company in the second half of the nineteenth century or the first half of the twentieth. I set out to confirm that hypothesis not because I really had much doubt about it but because I wanted to see whether a phenomenon like that could be traced with quantitative models.

And even when a model basically confirms a well-established hunch, we are likely to learn something along the way. In this case, the division I had expected to find turned out to be subtler and more complex than I began by assuming. Instead of Huyssen's emerging "gap between high art and mass culture," I found something more like a slight unfolding of previously parallel axes.[21] I can also say with considerable confidence now that the change was gradual. The evidence uncovered here might even allow a skeptic to raise questions about the theory I initially borrowed from Pierre Bourdieu. His assumption that economic and cultural capital can be treated as separate axes of distinction is clearly well suited to twentieth-century culture. But there could be some risk of anachronism in projecting it back onto a nineteenth-century cultural field where those aspects of prominence were less independent.

The Narrative Challenge of Long Timelines

If a divergence between prestige and popularity is something I expected to find at the outset of this project, most of this chapter's other conclusions are not. The standards governing literary reception are more stable than I expected: a model trained on evidence from one quarter century can make predictions that are almost equally good fifty years in the future. This holds true not just in the Victorian era (where we might expect stability) but across the advent of modernism, which has been widely char-

---

21. Huyssen, *After the Great Divide*, 194.

acterized as a literary "revolution."[22] Literary judgment is never easy to predict; the models described in this chapter range from only 72.5% to 83% accurate. But the part of reception that can be predicted at all is predicted by models that change relatively little from the 1850s through the 1940s. Moreover, a large component of the change that does take place appears to have a clear long-term social rationale. Poetry and fiction both move steadily in the direction of prevailing critical standards. Poetry apparently moves twice as fast as fiction. There may be a scholar somewhere who expected to see all this, but I confess that I didn't. I believed the histories that taught me to interpret the last two hundred years as a series of conflicts between roughly generational literary movements, separated by periods of stability.

Theory guides empirical inquiry, but new empirical results should also eventually reshape theory. So what theoretical inferences might we draw from this chapter's models of literary prestige? Our theoretical reflections needn't take the form of a new master narrative or causal explanation. We already have several of those, which we invoke at will depending on the problem we need to explain—talking sometimes about class conflict and ideology; sometimes about authors' individual aspirations; and sometimes about the jostling of institutions, technologies, and literary forms. If the tension between those alternative modes of explanation had been easy to resolve, we would have resolved it already. Historical change is a multifaceted thing, and I doubt quantitative methods will bring us much closer to a streamlined explanation.

On the other hand, when we discover unexpected evidence, we should pause to review our epistemological strategies, because some of them are probably responsible for the blind spot that has just been exposed. At this point in the book, it should be clear

22. Richard Fallis, "Yeats and the Reinterpretation of Victorian Poetry," *Victorian Poetry* 14, no. 2 (1976): 89–100; Stephen Greenblatt et al., eds., *Norton Anthology of English Literature*, 8th ed. (New York: W. W. Norton, 2006), 2:1834.

that literary scholars have had a blind spot. Our histories have explained literary change primarily by narrating short decadal or generational struggles, which we often treat as profound revolutions. We have said very little about slower processes that drift in the same direction for a century or more. Quantitative methods expose a different picture. There are still moments of sudden change in the picture: in chapter 2, for instance, we found that the detective story emerged just as suddenly as histories centered around Edgar Allan Poe have suggested. So numbers can reveal sudden changes, where history contains sudden changes. But numbers also reveal a host of slower changes that our existing histories have failed to describe. Chapter 1 demonstrated that literary history could be organized around a long differentiation of fiction from nonfiction narrative. This chapter has revealed that long arcs of that kind are not merely linguistic patterns or lines on a graph but coherent social processes. Some of the linguistic trends we encountered in chapter 1 (movement toward concrete language, for instance) now seem to have been enforced by the pressure of a particular, durable model of literary prestige.

Why did previous generations of critics fail to describe all this? A simple answer, true as far as it goes, is that critics in previous generations lacked computers and digital libraries. But the role of technology in opening new perspectives could be oversold. It is true that computers make this labor easier, but index cards can also work. When scholars really wanted to describe durable aspects of literary judgment, they found ways to do it by close-reading dozens of sample passages—as I. A. Richards does, for instance, in *Practical Criticism* (1929). It is true that a twenty-first-century imitator of Richards would be unlikely to find many readers, but in making that observation, we start to home in on the part of our blind spot that is theoretical rather than technological. The deeper problem is that, for the last sixty or seventy years, we have assumed that literary history can only be interesting and edifying insofar as it is a story about conflict.

An immense amount of ink has been spilled, for instance, on conflicts between Romanticism and realism, or between realism and experimental modernism. Those conflicts are real and worth discussion. But we have treated them as the whole story of literature, when they may be only half of it. When we back up to look at a bigger picture, the changes that become visible are not, as one might have expected, ripples and residual echoes of conflicts that had emerged a decade or two earlier at the high end of the market. Instead, we see the whole literary field move slowly in the same direction, guided by well-established, broadly shared standards. "Do people like poetic diction that's concrete and tinged with melancholy?" writers seem to reflect. "Very well, I'll write poetry that is concrete and melancholy—but even more so!" The historical power of "even more so" needs broader recognition than literary critics have given it. When we are reasoning cynically about genre fiction and movie pitches, we recognize the iron grip of this principle. "Even more so" explains how a single gritty reboot that makes money can doom us to a long sequence of ever-grittier reboots. But for some reason, historians of high literary forms have ignored that kind of momentum, preferring to suggest instead that change is driven by overt aesthetic debate or covert ideological conflict. To be clear: I am not denying that conflict plays a role in cultural history. But there are also such things as tacit assumptions that slowly intensify for many decades, precisely because they remain tacit.

Critics' tendency to ignore this form of change may emerge partly from their own rhetorical needs as writers: conflict simply makes a good story. A bias in favor of good stories may be unavoidable; I am not suggesting that we should give up storytelling. But our bias in favor of conflict is about more than narrative interest. There are also arbitrary theoretical assumptions at work: for instance, an implicit Hegelian model of change as dialectical struggle.

I like dialectical models myself. They are closely associated with a tradition of historical materialism that has done a great deal to illuminate the human past. But even cultural materialists need to consider the possibility that dialectic may not be the right explanation in every case and at every scale of description.

Sometimes the forward motion of a train has nothing to do with the people having a fistfight on top of it. Moreover, our reasons for focusing on the fistfight are not always as materialist as we pretend. It may be no accident, for instance, that literary historians have often chosen to emphasize generation-sized struggles. A perpetual dethroning of literary father figures satisfies the demands of Freudian agon as well as Marxist dialectic.[23]

But we can find other ways to narrate literary history. In particular, we need better ways to narrate slow change. Scholars are already aware that many aspects of literary judgment change slowly. In choosing exemplary works for syllabi, we tacitly acknowledge an axis of distinction that can outlast ephemeral movements and periods. But we keep this quality of exemplarity separate from the normative standards that organized a book's reception by its contemporaries. At any rate, we are not good at explaining how they intersect. Scholars whose research is characterized by a fiercely local historical relativism will switch gears suddenly when discussing syllabi in order to say that a book they have chosen is just better written in some timeless sense than an alternate example of the same movement. The Paterian notion that we are choosing an example "which expresses most adequately this or that special manifestation" of beauty has always made a thin cover story for the contradiction.[24] "Most adequately" by what yardstick, after all, if standards of judgment are mutable?

Instead of treating exemplarity as a principle separate from history, we need to develop a larger scale of historicism, able to acknowledge that our own aesthetic preferences are directly produced by and still implicated in the changes under discussion. This is a narrative problem as much a philosophical one, and I don't pretend to have completely solved it in this chapter. Part of the challenge is simply to trace an arc long enough to connect the twenty-first century to the nineteenth or eighteenth. If we want

23. The Freudian agon becomes explicit, of course, in Harold Bloom, *The Anxiety of Influence: A Theory of Poetry*, 2nd ed. (New York: Oxford University Press, 1997), 9–10.

24. Walter Pater, *The Renaissance; Studies in Art and Poetry*, 2nd ed. (London: Macmillan, 1877), vii–viii.

to cover that span of time without speculative hand waving, statistical models are helpful. But statistical models of the past are not produced simply by pressing a button. The models developed in this chapter were limited to 130 years because they required social as well as textual evidence, and gathering the evidence proved to be a great deal of work even with the help of collaborators. I am sure that larger teams will find it possible to organize better data sets about sales and literary reviewing.

Moreover, quantitative models still have to be interpreted, and the interpretation of literary models will depend to some extent on attentive reading of particular works and passages. In this chapter, the criteria that governed poetic distinction could be described adequately in semantic terms alone. (Concrete description of the natural world contrasts clearly enough against abstract description of social life.) But when it came to fiction, the criteria of prestige were not wholly intelligible as a list of words or semantic categories. To understand that model, we had to consider how words were actually used in stories, and I only scratched the surface of what could be said on the topic.

In short, this chapter claims to expose a problem in our current approach to literary history. If I am right, an important component of change spreads out across a longer arc than our theories and narrative strategies have been able to reveal. But I don't claim to have resolved the problem, either intellectually or as a matter of narrative craft. Statistical models can help us understand the social forces shaping a long arc of literary change. But turning those models into fully satisfying stories could take several more decades. In this chapter, for instance, I have only lightly touched on the interplay of market success with different kinds of prestige. Whole books could be written to explore that topic. Those books will have to be written and reviewed and critiqued before we can say that we fully understand the transformation of literature across a long timeline.

After that foundation has been laid, we may be able to write more satisfying historical narratives. In this chapter I have switched abruptly from one scale of description to another: using a model to characterize the social coherence of a whole century and then plunging into close analysis of a few plaintive lines from Christina Rossetti. I can imagine a more flexible mode of narration that would trace different wavelengths of change using models of different sizes. A literary historian might close-read passages not just to illustrate the models but to explain transitions between them. In a story of that kind, individual writers would become significant figures in a long procession. They would be neither unique outliers nor merely examples of a type but agents embodying the sweep and pathos of a larger process, like characters in a historical novel—if historical novels had graphs.

But narratives of that kind may have to emerge from a process almost as slow and collective as literary history itself. The introductions to our anthologies didn't acquire their casual confidence overnight; they are condensed summaries that build on two centuries of bibliography and debate. New quantitative methods will initially disrupt that confidence, reopen debate, and create aesthetic problems for literary historians. We may have to spend another decade or two checking our assumptions and getting our facts right before we are ready to put things back together again in a composed and elegant way.

4

Metamorphoses of Gender

Although the foregoing chapters of this book have occasionally paused to read a passage closely, they have mostly discussed volumes of poetry or fiction as wholes. Across a two- or three-century timeline, that level of abstraction is useful, revealing historical patterns otherwise invisible. But readers don't experience works of literature as unified data points. In reading fiction, our attention is directed less to the work as a verbal object than to the imaginary places, people, and events inside it. In fact, students who are writing about literature for the first time often ignore the mediation of the text altogether in order to discuss fictional characters as if they were real.

Historians of literature obviously need a bit more distance from fiction. But we also want to connect our history to readers' experience—which means that we need some way of connecting historical trends to the imaginary people and events inside the volumes. This was relatively easy as long as we were working with a repertoire of forty or sixty books commonly taken to represent (say) the Victorian novel. We could just point to Heathcliff or Maggie Tulliver. But in a century-spanning story covering thousands of works, it becomes difficult to pretend that a few characters are representative. We need some way of reasoning collectively about hundreds of thousands of fictional people.

This chapter takes a few steps in that direction, in order to trace the history of gender roles in English-language fiction from 1780 to the present. But even a few steps toward a history of character will admittedly take us to the edge of what is now possible. The methods discussed here are more complex than those discussed in earlier chapters, the evidence often a little noisier. Some aspects of character will simply get left out. Here, for instance, is an example of what natural language processing learns about Maggie Tulliver, from a few sentences in *The Mill on the Floss*. By connecting pronouns to the name "Maggie," and verbs to pronouns, a computer can learn that the italicized words below are things Maggie does or attributes she possesses.

> The resolute din, the unresting motion of the great stones, giving her a dim delicious *awe* as at the presence of an uncontrollable force— the meal forever pouring, pouring—the fine white powder softening all surfaces, and making the very spider-nets look like a faery lace-work—the sweet pure scent of the meal—all helped to make Maggie *feel* that the mill was a little world apart from her outside every-day *life*. The spiders were especially a subject of speculation with her. She *wondered* if they had any relatives outside the mill.[1]

Our methods are blind to a great deal in this passage: for instance, the spiderwebs look "like a faery lace-work" *to* Maggie, so that imaginative simile should probably inflect our understanding of her character. But the algorithm I am using doesn't model point of view. It sees only that Maggie has *awe* and a *life*, and that she *feels* and *wonders*. And yet, sketchy as those details are, they aren't a terrible summary of what we learn about Maggie from these sentences. If we extend these same methods across the whole book, we can come away with a decent rough sketch of its characters. If we apply the same methods to hundreds of thousands of books, we may begin to recognize patterns of change.

To do this, I'll use a software tool called BookNLP, written by my collaborator David Bamman, who fundamentally shaped

---

1. George Eliot, *The Mill on the Floss*, 3 vols. (Edinburgh: William Blackwood, 1860), 1:45–46.

much of the research described in this chapter.[2] Works of fiction can refer to characters in several different ways—using proper nouns, but also pronouns and common nouns. BookNLP starts with proper nouns, clustering names so that "Maggie" and "Maggie Tulliver" are linked as a single person. Then it identifies pronouns that refer back to those names and adds their syntactic dependencies to a model of Miss Tulliver. The final model includes the adjectives that modify a character, the nouns they possess, and verbs that describe actions performed by or on the character. (We know, for instance, that Maggie *saw*, but Stephen Guest *was seen*.) This system will capture most of what is said about most characters, but it does have some acknowledged blind spots. In using only proper names to identify characters, we miss out on characters who are exclusively referred to in generic terms, such as "the footman." Uncommon nicknames (such as "Pip" for Philip Pirrip) may result in a single character being divided into multiple roles.

In short, BookNLP does not always draw the boundaries of identity where a human reader would draw them. Gender, on the other hand, is comparatively easy to recognize. Even when a single character is split into multiple roles, BookNLP usually assigns gender to each role correctly, guided by names and honorifics ("Mr," "Lady," "Miss"). First-person narrators constitute a significant exception because there are no signs of gender attached to the pronoun "I." So first-person narrators won't be included in this chapter's story; further research will be needed to determine if they have a different history. Where other characters are concerned, BookNLP assigns gender with reasonable accuracy. Most importantly for the diachronic questions we want to pose, accuracy seems to be relatively stable over time, at least from 1800 forward.[3]

2. David Bamman, Ted Underwood, and Noah Smith, "A Bayesian Mixed Effects Model of Literary Character," *ACL 2014*, accessed 2014, http://www.cs.cmu.edu/~ark/literaryCharacter/.

3. Questions of accuracy can be subdivided in a variety of ways. Researchers often distinguish "precision" (how many instances the model flagged as X were really X) from

This foundation is solid enough to sketch some broad patterns affecting the representation of gender over the last two hundred years. But the patterns unveiled in this chapter may at first look paradoxical. Two trends point apparently in opposite directions. The first is that gender divisions between characters have become less predictable. In the middle of the nineteenth century, very different language is used to describe fictional men and women. But that difference weakens steadily as we move forward to the present; the actions and attributes of characters are less clearly sorted into gender categories. This may sound like a progressive story: a character's role in a narrative is increasingly independent of his or her public gender identity. But the second trend this chapter will describe points in a different direction. If we trace the sheer space on the page allotted to women, we discover a startling decline both in the number of characters who are women or girls and in the percentage of a text writers devote to describing them. In short, while gender roles were becoming more flexible, the attention actually devoted to women was declining. If we look more closely at the details of this story, however, the paradox may be only apparent. We may even begin to understand how both trends could emerge from the same underlying cause.

Modeling Implicit Gender Roles

This chapter considers both the gender positions ascribed to authors as biographical personages and the signs of gender they use in producing characters. In both cases, we will discuss "masculinity" and "femininity" as conventional roles people were expected to assume in order to become legible in a social context. Other roles are certainly possible, but this chapter doesn't pretend to cover gender exhaustively. It is a history mainly of the binary

"recall" (how many of the real Xs the model identified). BookNLP identifies women with 94.7% precision / 83.1% recall and men with 91.3% precision / 85.7% recall. For further discussion, especially of diachronic variation in error rates, see Ted Underwood, "Data and Code to Support *Distant Horizons*," last modified December 7, 2017, https://github.com/tedunderwood/horizon/tree/master/chapter4/error.

scheme that dominated public representation of gender from the late eighteenth century through the end of the twentieth. This history will cast light on more complex forms of identification only indirectly, by showing that even binary signs of gender could mean different things at different times or to different observers. To begin with, we can ask how strongly public signs of gender shaped characterization in general. Were fictive men quite different from fictive women, or were the differences between characters mostly unrelated to conventional signs of gender? And how did the answer to that question vary across the timeline?

Questions about the relative strength of different relationships are a place where quantitative methods shine. But we can't know in advance which aspects of character might be surreptitiously gendered. A wide range of actions (speaking, smiling, even walking) might be associated implicitly with one gender or another. We need a capacious way of representing many different aspects of character at once in order to ask how well gender explains them collectively. A bag-of-words representation has worked well for many similar problems. We represent each character by the adjectives that modify them, the verbs they govern, and so on—excluding only words that explicitly name a gendered role like *boyhood* or *wife*. Then we present characters, labeled with grammatical gender, to a learning algorithm. The algorithm will learn what it means to be "masculine" or "feminine" purely by observing what men and women actually do in stories. The model produced by the algorithm can make predictions about other characters, previously unseen. If these predictions are very accurate, we can conclude that fictive men and women are very different: almost every aspect of character seems to provide a reliable clue about gender. In periods where the model becomes less accurate, we might conclude that gender was a less pervasive organizing structure—or at least that gender was being expressed in ways that didn't align predictably with the binary division between *he* and *she*.

When we attempt this comparison, a clear long-term pattern emerges: the differences between male and female characters get

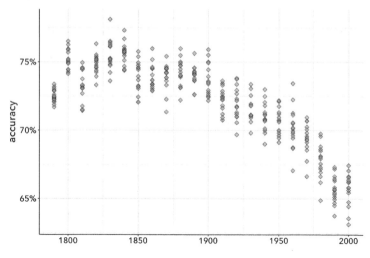

FIGURE 4.1. Accuracy of models predicting the gender of characters. Each data point reflects the accuracy of a particular model trained to distinguish eight hundred men and eight hundred women, sampled randomly from a larger collection of characters in a given period.

steadily less predictable from the middle of the nineteenth century to the beginning of the twenty-first.

The diamonds in figure 4.1 are arranged in columns because we ran fifteen different models in each decade, randomly selecting sixteen hundred characters each time and classifying them using the twenty-two hundred most common words in that group of characters. To make these comparisons apples to apples, we ensured that the median "size" of the text associated with characters was roughly fifty-four words in every decade. That's not a lot of words (many characters are described fairly briefly), so these models are never as accurate as a model of genre (which uses a whole volume for each inference). Genre models often exceed 90% accuracy; these character models peak around 77% and bottom out around 64%.

The characters used for this analysis come from a collection of 93,960 volumes drawn from HathiTrust Digital Library. Collected mostly by American academic libraries (along with public institutions like the Library of Congress), this library is by no means a complete record of fiction published in English. Later in the chapter, we will consider some of its limitations and compare it to several other samples. But the major limitation of all libraries, where gender is concerned, is very simple: men wrote more of the books than women. Since gender is a perspectival category, we will often want to separate books by men and books by women in order to ask how they represent gender differently. For instance, we could produce two different versions of figure 4.1, one trained only on characters invented by men, the other trained only on characters invented by women. When I do this, I get two different versions of the same arc—perfectly parallel, and one slightly below the other. Gender boundaries are consistently more predictable in books by men, across the whole timeline we are considering. Gender is consistently harder to infer in books written by women. In a few pages, we will ask what might produce this difference, but for the moment I want to focus on the similarity. Diachronically, these two arcs have the same shape: whether we look at books written by men or women, gender gets steadily harder to infer from (roughly) 1840 to the present.

Before running this test, I asked myself what I would expect to see, and a downward slope of some kind is certainly what I expected. We know that the nineteenth-century doctrine of "separate spheres" defined the home as a feminine domain and the public sphere as masculine. As the doctrine of separate spheres was challenged and women moved into careers previously closed to them, we might expect gender roles to become less crisply distinguished, both inside and outside the covers of a novel.[4] Before 1850, patterns of change are less clear, both because we have fewer data points and because I have noticed that the trend in this part of the timeline is fairly sensitive to modeling assumptions. But if there were a slight increase in accuracy from 1780 to 1840, it would fit received narratives about the rise of domestic

4. See, for instance, Monika M. Elbert, ed., *Separate Spheres No More: Gender Convergence in American Literature* (Tuscaloosa: University of Alabama Press, 2000).

ideology reasonably well. Virginia Woolf, at any rate, believed that "the sexes drew further and further apart" as the nineteenth century began.[5]

In short, I think it may be relatively easy to understand the arc in figure 4.1. Explanations for it are handy. On the other hand, it would be an overstatement to say that "we already knew" the shape of the arc. In truth, we don't know it even now. Other projects using similar methods have reached different conclusions. For instance, Matthew Jockers and Gabi Kirilloff found little change in the gendering of verbs in nineteenth-century fiction.[6] And in fact, if we could only examine evidence from the nineteenth century, it might be reasonable to conclude that gender roles have been largely stable across time. Most of the decline revealed in figure 4.1 comes in the twentieth century. That important detail is by no means self-evident in our critical narratives. Some stories about modernism imply that it reversed nineteenth-century progress for women; other narratives describe a significant period of backsliding in the 1940s and 1950s.[7] If those reversals took place, they don't become visible in figure 4.1. In short, even when a quantitative result roughly confirms one plausible set of expectations, it doesn't mean that we already had consensus on the topic. This result may support certain tacit assumptions about the history of gender, but writers have made many different assumptions about that history.

In fact, I expect researchers will continue to disagree about the curve in figure 4.1. Excluding certain gendered words as "tautological" clues is a debatable move because it is not obvious where

5. Virginia Woolf, *Orlando: A Biography*, ed. Rachel Bowlby (Oxford: Oxford University Press, 1992), 219.

6. Matthew Jockers and Gabi Kirilloff, "Understanding Gender and Character Agency in the 19th Century Novel," *Cultural Analytics*, December 1, 2016, http://culturalanalytics.org/2016/12/understanding-gender-and-character-agency-in-the-19th-century-novel/.

7. Suzanne Clark, *Sentimental Modernism: Women Writers and the Revolution of the Word* (Bloomington: Indiana University Press, 1991), 1; Gayle Greene, *Changing the Story: Feminist Fiction and the Tradition* (Bloomington: Indiana University Press, 1991), 39–41.

to stop. We may agree that *he* and *she* convey nothing but a gender signal. References to a character's *boyhood* are almost as clear. But *husband* and *wife* are more debatable cases. In this data set, most of the characters with wives will be men, but that really depends on sexuality rather than gender. Probably the best solution would be to exclude gendered relationship terms as predicates (since "Mr Darcy was her husband" conveys Darcy's gender tautologically) but not as attributes possessed by the character (since possession of a husband signals Elizabeth's gender only if she happens to be heterosexual). In some modeling runs we made that distinction, but not in the final version represented above. Nor did we exclude references to the body or articles of dress, although skirts and mustaches are arguably signs of gender.

These fine lines are interesting philosophically, and they will make a difference when critics start arguing about subtle inflections of the curve. But the debatable cases make little difference to the biggest historical pattern: the broad decline in accuracy from 1840 to 2007. I worked on this project for three years, collaborating with David Bamman and Sabrina Lee; we tested that decline using a range of different assumptions, different code, and different sources of data. Although figure 4.1 relies entirely on HathiTrust, we initially used novels from the Chicago Text Lab in the twentieth century; we found broadly the same pattern in that collection. Finally, we tested the reliability of BookNLP's gender inference by comparing the predicted gender to manual judgments for 525 characters evenly distributed over time to make sure the perceived decline in accuracy wasn't merely a decline in the reliability of our ground truth. In short, the blurring of gender boundaries from 1840 through the late twentieth century is a robust trend; it is not likely to vanish with a different set of sampling or modeling choices.

So why did it happen? In a sense, we already know. The underlying social forces that made gender roles more flexible are not a deep mystery: we can make a shrewd guess that roles changed as women moved into a wider range of wage-earning professions and eventually won the vote. Causal explanation, in this case,

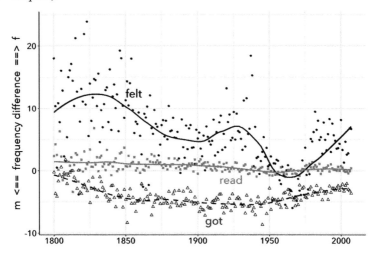

FIGURE 4.2. Gendering of *felt*, *read*, and *got*. For each word, its frequency in five thousand words describing men is subtracted from its frequency in five thousand words describing women.

may not be the difficult part of the problem. The question more likely to interest literary historians is *how exactly* fictional roles were transformed by those social trends. What were the patterns that made characters easy to sort by gender around 1840, and how did those patterns change? There are many ways to pose that question. For instance, we trained a series of predictive models to produce figure 4.1; we could crack open those models and reason about coefficients. But in a complex model, coefficients can be tricky to interpret. Let's try a simpler approach: if we calculate a word's frequency in characterization of women and subtract its frequency in characterization of men, we'll have a simple measure of its importance as a gender signal. Words with a big positive difference will convey femininity; those with a negative difference will convey masculinity. This measure tends to emphasize common words, but for our purposes that's fine: we want to find changes that were big enough to make gender hard to infer. Figure 4.2, for instance, shows the frequency of three common verbs.

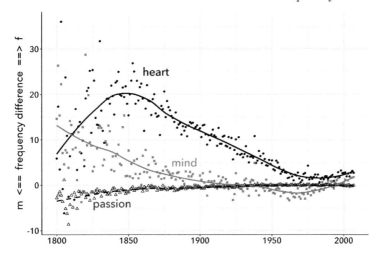

FIGURE 4.3. Gendering of *heart*, *mind*, and *passion*. Each word's frequency in descriptions of women, minus its frequency in descriptions of men.

Reading is an action that fictional men and women perform equally often, and that balance stays pretty equal across two centuries of fiction. But *got* is governed more often by a masculine subject and *felt* by a feminine one. However, the surplus of feminine feeling declines as we move forward on the timeline, either because *felt* was used more often to describe men or because it was used less often to describe everyone (this graph doesn't try to separate those changes). There's even a brief period in the 1960s when the word is used more often for men.

We're looking for words like *felt*—words that created a lot of gender differentiation early in this period but less toward the end. Words with that kind of arc might explain why the language used to describe character became (on the whole) less gendered over time. Instead of choosing words at random, we can sort them to find words that move toward the central dividing line. When we do, we come up with words like the ones in figure 4.3.

Language of subjective consciousness and feeling, in general, was gendered female in the nineteenth century. This is true not only for *heart* (and *tears* and *sighs* and *smiles*), as we might expect,

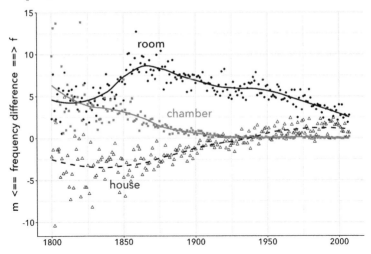

FIGURE 4.4. Gendering of *room*, *chamber*, and *house*. Each word's frequency in descriptions of women, minus its frequency in descriptions of men.

but for less emotive terms like *mind* and *spirits*. There are only a few subjective nouns ascribed more often to men; the primary one is *passion*, which is sometimes a nineteenth-century euphemism for lust. If we're concerned about the difference between *mind* (verb) and *mind* (noun), by the way, BookNLP does allow us to separate them. In practice, this pattern is so dominated by the noun that separation would make little difference.

The pattern we are seeing here is loosely congruent with Nancy Armstrong's well-known thesis that subjectivity was to begin with "a female domain" in the novel: "It was at first only women," she says, "who were defined in terms of their emotional natures."[8] Only as we move toward the middle of the nineteenth century does psychological depth become equally important for male characters; in Armstrong's narrative, this shift is dramatized with a reading of Heathcliff in *Wuthering Heights*.

The evidence in figure 4.4 also supports Armstrong's conten-

8. Nancy Armstrong, *Desire and Domestic Fiction: A Political History of the Novel* (New York: Oxford University Press, 1987), 4. Andrew Piper has recently given this thesis an interesting twist by emphasizing that the interiority of feminine characters is especially marked for "female protagonists by female novelists." Piper, *Enumerations*, 122.

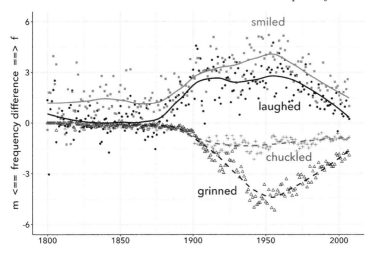

FIGURE 4.5. Gendering of *laughed, smiled, grinned,* and *chuckled.* Each word's frequency in descriptions of women, minus its frequency in descriptions of men.

tion that the gendering of privacy and interiority was linked to a broader division between public and domestic spaces. In early-nineteenth-century novels, men have houses and countries. Women have private chambers and apartments inside the house, and once that language becomes old fashioned, they have rooms. But this differentiation of spaces slowly declines across two centuries. By the later twentieth century, in fact, the house is associated slightly more often with women. (This could reflect the decline of coverture, allowing women to share legal ownership of a house—or perhaps also a growing sense that the whole suburban dwelling counts as private domestic space.)

These familiar changes go some distance toward explaining the growing blurriness of gender boundaries. But growing blurriness is not the only story one can tell with this evidence. In fact, there is far more going on in the data than I could completely describe in one chapter. I am highlighting long-term trends, but a close observer will also notice fascinating little stories by the wayside. Some of these involve the creation of new forms of gender differentiation. For instance, figure 4.5 shows that verbs of mirth become strongly gendered in the middle of the twentieth century.

Women smile and laugh, but midcentury men, apparently, can only grin and chuckle. I cannot fully explain this weird twentieth-century behavior, but it is interesting that the feminization of the common verbs *smile* and *laugh* seems to have preceded the development of masculine alternatives—almost as though it became inappropriate for fictive men to smile once fictive women were doing it so much. This gendering of mirth peaks in the years before and after World War II, and Raymond Chandler is a typical expression of its consequences for men. His male characters have a habit of grinning in an uneasy laconic way. "He grinned. His teeth had a freckled look." Or: "He grinned. His dentist was tired of waiting for him."[9] Chandler's grins are commonly followed by a cynical chaser about the character's appearance, to make clear that masculine humor is a thin veneer stretched over menace.

These expressions of gender can be periodized and dated because they are on their way out now. But other expressions of gender have continued to expand. In particular, description of the human body becomes steadily more important in fiction. Ryan Heuser and Long Le-Khac have shown that this is a broad, steady trend; it is, of course, part of the growing emphasis on physical description traced in chapters 1 and 3.[10] And as writers spent more time describing their characters physically, those physical descriptions also became more specifically gendered. A whole article could be written on this topic: jaws, hands, lips, and feet are all fascinating. But Figure 4.6 illustrates a few leading examples.

There are actually several different waves of physical description. The top curve for *eyes* is emblematic of several other terms that peak in the late nineteenth century. Many of these involve the feminine head: *lips, eyes, face,* and *voice* are all associated with women. Then these powerful signs decline, making way for later waves of gendered physical description that become important in

9. Raymond Chandler, in *The World of Raymond Chandler: In His Own Words*, ed. Barry Day (New York: Penguin Random House, 2014), 211.

10. Heuser and Le-Khac, "Quantitative Literary History."

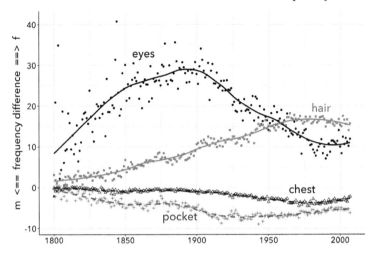

FIGURE 4.6. Gendering of *eyes, hair, chest,* and *pocket*. Each word's frequency in descriptions of women, minus its frequency in descriptions of men.

the twentieth century. Many of these involve the body or clothes. The masculine chest slowly becomes important, although bodily description is never quite as central for men as it is for women. (*Body* itself, in fact, is gendered feminine.) One of the main things men do have is a pocket; in the twentieth century they are constantly putting things in it. At present, hair is one of the most powerful signifiers of femininity.

So pulling all this together, what can we conclude? Some forms of gender differentiation (associated for instance with domestic space and subjectivity) are declining, while other forms (associated for instance with the body and clothes) are on the rise. If we add them all together, we can say generally that gender is less insistently marked by the end of the twentieth century than it was in the 1840s. But that slow increase in blurriness could be less important than the churn we have seen along the way: the rise and fall of different forms of gender differentiation. Although the opposition of *he* and *she* remains grammatically the same, gender is actually quite a different thing by 2007 than it had been in 1840.

So far we have considered books in the aggregate, in order to show, for instance, that gender roles become less predictable as time passes. But there were in reality huge differences between books and authors at every point on the timeline. How significant is the historical trend relative to the variation between works? To answer that question, we need a way to place individual books on a graph. But we can't train a separate model of gender for each book; there won't be enough data to make those models meaningful.

What we can do is measure the gap between the probability of being feminine predicted for a book's fictional women and its fictional men, using a model of gender defined by other works from the same period. This will tell us, in effect, how much gender dimorphism we are seeing in a given volume. If characters conform very clearly to gender roles prevailing in the period, our model will give the book's women a high probability of femininity and its men a low probability. If gender roles are less stereotyped, there will be a smaller gap. In figure 4.7, I have plotted the difference between masculine and feminine means for six titles, as well as for a collection of twentieth-century science fiction, and for all books by authors who were men, or women.

Readers may notice first of all that the vertical axis only reaches up to about 8%: the perceived difference between genders is never very large. That's because our data for any single character are sparse, and well-tuned models make cautious predictions about sparse data. So even a stereotypically masculine character may be ascribed a 45% probability of being feminine. In this environment, a 10% difference between men and women is, relatively speaking, a sign of stark gender polarity. In 93,960 volumes from HathiTrust Digital Library, the average difference between genders starts out around 7% and declines to around 3%. This decline broadly echoes the arc we saw in figure 4.1: those models became less accurate precisely because masculine and feminine characters were growing harder to separate. We also see a pattern I mentioned earlier: gender divisions are consistently stronger in books written by men. The models used to create figure 4.7 were

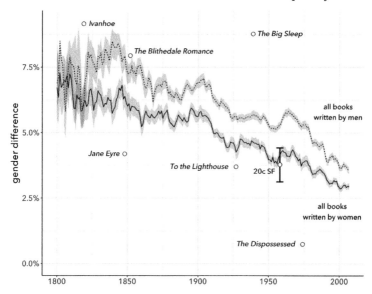

FIGURE 4.7. Gender dimorphism in characterization, 1800–2000. A different model of femininity is trained for each half century. We calculate the weighted mean probability for (actual) women and subtract the mean probability for (actual) men to assess the implicit gap separating genders in a given book or year. Trend lines are smoothed with a three-year moving window and surrounded with a 95% confidence interval.

trained on all authors, but if we modeled books written by men and women separately, we would see the same pattern: gendered behavior is consistently more legible in books written by men.

Statistical analysis of individual volumes casts some light on this pattern. It turns out that women are consistently under-represented in books by men. On average, only a third of the words men use in characterization are used to describe feminine characters. Women writers, on the other hand, spend equal time on fictional men and fictional women. This difference remains depressingly constant across two centuries, and it may help explain why books by men tend to have more stereotyped gender roles. Gender dimorphism of the kind plotted in figure 4.7 tends to be higher in books where women are underrepresented

(r = .258). This may happen in part because the lonely woman in a Western or hard-boiled detective story is likely to be depicted in a deeply gendered way. She becomes, in effect, "The Woman." We might call this the Irene Adler Distortion, if Katha Politt hadn't already memorably dubbed it "the Smurfette Principle."[11] Admittedly, this principle doesn't fully explain male writers' obsession with gender. If we compare books by men and women with similar fractions of female characters, the books by men will still have slightly starker gender polarities. In short, everything affects everything: as usual with statistics, there is no single cause. But the underrepresentation of women in books by men may be one reason for the stark gender dimorphism in those books.

To explore a less depressing pattern, we could consider the relation between representation of gender and literary prestige. The reviewed authors discussed in chapter 3 have (on average) a gender gap slightly smaller than usual for their date of publication. This pattern holds from 1850 to 1950, and it seems to get stronger with time. Books reviewed in prestigious venues are increasingly less likely to describe their characters in conventionally gendered ways. But this effect is not very strong (r = −.151). Up to 1950, at least, the gender of an author makes a bigger difference than his or her critical reception.

Genre also, surprisingly, doesn't matter as much as one might assume. I have investigated detective stories, Westerns, romances, and works of science fiction. Although the role of gender in characterization does vary from one genre to the next, it does so, for the most part, roughly as one might predict from the gender identification of the authors themselves. Characters in Westerns are more clearly gendered than usual (but not much more clearly than one would predict for books written by men). Characters in romances are less clearly gendered (but about average for books written by women). This result for romances will perhaps sound surprising, since gothic romances of the late twentieth century have sometimes been accused of foregrounding and reinforcing

11. Katha Politt, "Hers; The Smurfette Principle," *New York Times*, April 7, 1991.

conventional gender roles. But the evidence I have seen suggests that gender boundaries in romance are less predictable than in, say, Westerns. A few male-dominated subgenres are notable outliers. Hard-boiled detective novels by male writers are some of the most insistently gendered books in the twentieth century. Raymond Chandler and Dashiell Hammett both float to the top of the list. The patterns that put them there are precisely what a reader of those stories might expect: a cast of tough guys and manipulative, deceptive women. The patterns are legible even in the condensed output produced by BookNLP. Carmen Sternwood, in *The Big Sleep*, "bubbles," "smiles," "giggles" repeatedly, and then "shoots" at the protagonist. Her "eyes" and "face" are frequently mentioned. Certain kinds of pulp adventure fiction are also profoundly gendered. In the Tarzan books of Edgar Rice Burroughs, male and female characters are divided by a gap of as much as 20%; the gender polarity in these books is every bit as stark as the proverbial opposition "me Tarzan, you Jane" might suggest.

It would be tempting to make fun of these pulpy examples, but I want to be careful not to imply that the vertical axis in figure 4.7 is measuring political virtue. Although *Jane Eyre* is positioned in a way that makes Charlotte Brontë look ahead of her time, as one might expect, a novel like *The Mill on the Floss*—actually a powerful feminist critique—comes out about average for its era. But it would be a mistake to imagine that this calculation reveals anything damning about George Eliot. To judge a book's political implications, it is of course not sufficient to ask whether its characters do or don't (collectively) conform to the period's gender expectations. One needs to investigate the narrator's attitude to different characters and their struggle with the social environment depicted in the book.

The same kind of careful reflection is necessary as we back up to consider whole genres. For instance, gender is not a particularly prominent organizing principle of characterization in science fiction. The error bar plotted in figure 4.7 defines a 95% confidence interval for the difference between the average masculine character and the average feminine character. (Note that this is not representing the full range of science fiction volumes but our uncertainty about the *mean* difference between genders. The error bar is located at 1958 because that was the average date of publication for the eighty-seven volumes of twentieth-century science fiction I analyzed.) The mean difference between characters (3.8%) is not unusually low for books written by women. But of course, most twentieth-century books of science fiction were not written by women! The vast majority of these eighty-seven volumes were written by men, and the gap between characters is significantly smaller than we would expect for such a male-dominated genre.

This evidence need not necessarily imply that science fiction is progressive on the topic of gender. Women are as badly under-represented inside science-fictional universes as they are in most books by male authors. Probably the conclusion to be drawn is rather that science fiction has long been inclined to ignore gender. On the other hand, interesting possibilities may be latent in that blindness. Radical revisions of gender like Le Guin's *Left Hand of Darkness* (1969) and Ann Leckie's *Ancillary Justice* (2013) emerge from an underlying flexibility in science fiction that becomes, perhaps, more comprehensible in figure 4.7.

Of course, the flexibility of science fiction also marks a limit case for this analysis, since characters are often named and defined in ways that resist categorization. Books like *The Left Hand of Darkness* and, for that matter, Virginia Woolf's *Orlando* (1928) are exploring the limits of gender as a concept, not simply shrinking a gap between predefined roles. More broadly, all conclusions about individual books need to be treated with caution. Transcription errors in the digital text can confuse BookNLP more than most other methods used in this volume; even a dropped quotation mark, for instance, can be significant here. Running this analysis on slightly different copies of the same book will produce different results. If it weren't visually distracting, all the circles plotted for volumes in figure 4.7 would be accompanied by error bars larger than those associated with science fiction. Slight differences between individual volumes should not be taken very seriously. On the other hand, when we back up to consider tens of thousands of volumes across two hundred years, errors largely cancel each other out, and a collective pattern becomes visible. The steady dwindling of the gap separating fictional women and men is all the more interesting because it stands in tension with the durable gap between men and women as authors. This evidence almost seems to be saying: "Gender itself may be a volatile construct, but when it comes to acknowledging the volatility, women writers are consistently twenty-five years ahead of men." That would be a self-contradictory statement, to be sure, but it may be a contradiction worth exploring.

The Masculinization of Fiction, 1850–1970

This chapter began at the deep end of the pool, studying the strength of implicit gender boundaries. To measure a subtle and implicit dimension of character, we needed complex statistical methods. But we can also pose simpler questions about gender. For instance, what proportion of fictional characters are actually identified as women or girls?

The shrinking gap between masculine and feminine roles seen in the first half of the chapter might lead us to predict a similarly upbeat pattern here, with the prominence of women slowly increasing across the nineteenth and twentieth centuries. To be sure, we might expect some interruptions in that trend. There is a notorious backlash against first-wave feminism in the middle of the twentieth century, for instance—dated by Gayle Greene to the 1940s and 1950s.[12] But we might hope at least to see an overall story of progress across two centuries. If we were feeling cynical, we might predict stability. Perhaps the underrepresentation of women in fiction is a durable problem, largely unaffected by growing flexibility on an ideological level.

12. Greene, *Changing the Story*, 39–41.

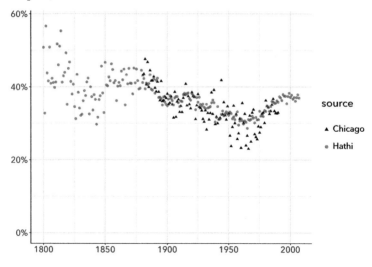

FIGURE 4.8. Percentage of words used in characterization that describe women. Words used to describe women, as a fraction of all words used to describe men or women.

If we start with either of those expectations, we will be disappointed. In fact, the prominence of women steadily declines in English-language fiction from the middle of the nineteenth century to the middle of the twentieth. In figure 4.8, I have plotted the proportion of words used in characterization that describe women. "Words used in characterization" here includes verbs a character governed and nouns they possessed (like "spirits"), as well as adjectives that modify a character. Dialogue spoken by characters is not counted, but including it would not materially change the pattern; nor would counting the characters themselves. Characters of unknown gender have been excluded from the total here, but including them wouldn't change the trend. However one measures it, the space allotted to women declines from the middle of the nineteenth century to the middle of the twentieth—in the very period when we might expect to see the effects of first-wave feminism. The trend reverses around 1970, for reasons we will investigate later.

This picture is counterintuitive enough that my first instinct was to ask whether it might be an artifact of some error in my collection or methods. Could there be some distortion in the way I selected volumes? One check is provided by the fact that figure 4.8 plots volumes from two different sources. The HathiTrust fiction corpus was separated from nonfiction algorithmically and includes one copy of every title that the algorithm tagged as fiction (including works in translation and folktales, for instance). The Chicago Novel Corpus was selected manually and includes only novels composed in English, emphasizing American works identified as prominent. Although I attempted a rough deduplication of HathiTrust, the Chicago corpus is also less likely to include duplicates and is far better at dating works by their date of first publication. (That is probably why the decline looks a bit steeper in the Chicago data.) But these differently constructed corpora display broadly the same pattern of gender inequality in characterization.

In short, this is a real trend. But how can we explain a trend that runs directly against our assumptions about social progress? One answer is that, during the period when women were becoming less prominent as characters in fiction, women *writers* were also losing shelf space in libraries. As mentioned above, women invent grammatically feminine characters much more often than men do, so any decline in the number of women writers will create a corresponding decline in description of women. And figure 4.9 shows that there was, in fact, a fairly stunning decline in the proportion of fiction writers who were women from the middle of the nineteenth century to the middle of the twentieth.

Women go from representing almost half the authors of fiction to less than a quarter. If this trend is real, it is an important fact about literary history that ought to be foregrounded even, say, in anthology introductions. But the story has not been widely publicized. There are some existing works of scholarship that highlight pieces of the decline. The most important of these is *Edging Women Out* (1989), where Gaye Tuchman and Nina Fortin report that "before 1840 at least half of all novelists were women; by 1917 most high-culture novelists were men." (This book remains a good rhetorical template for contemporary distant readers, by the way—weaving regression models and case studies very effectively

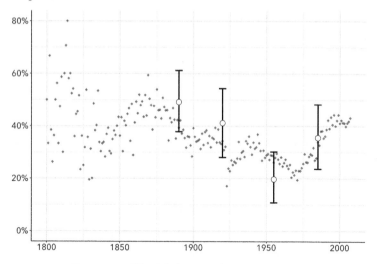

FIGURE 4.9. Percentage of English-language fiction titles written by women in HathiTrust (points) and *Publishers Weekly* (error bars). Reprints and books for a juvenile audience have been excluded.

into a single narrative.)[13] Separately, scholars of modernism have traced a redefinition of high culture that tended to disadvantage women. Suzanne Clark has explained that "modernism reversed the increasing influence of women's writing" by defining itself against the sentimental tradition.[14] But it is telling that Clark interprets this shift as a reversal of nineteenth-century progress for women, whereas Tuchman and Fortin see a story of nineteenth-century decline. It appears that scholars of each period are able to see the possibility that female authorship was declining in their own period. But no one has been willing to advance the dismal suggestion that the whole story from 1850 to 1970 was a story of decline.[15] Franco Moretti suggested that the appar-

---

13. Gaye Tuchman with Nina E. Fortin, *Edging Women Out: Victorian Novelists, Publishers, and Social Change* (London: Routledge, 2012), 7, 140.

14. Clark, *Sentimental Modernism*, 1.

15. Chris Forster may have been the first person to see that there is a larger story to tell here. Chris Forster, "A Walk through the Metadata: Gender in the HathiTrust Dataset," September 8, 2015, http://cforster.com/2015/09/gender-in-hathitrust-dataset/.

ent late-nineteenth-century decline might just be one phase of a cyclical pattern.[16] Nor has everyone agreed that the evidence for decline is persuasive even in the late nineteenth century. Ellen Miller Casey examined late-nineteenth-century reviews in the *Athenaeum* and concluded that "there is little evidence of a steady male invasion edging women out."[17]

So how trustworthy is our own evidence? There are two reasons for skepticism. One is that novels in HathiTrust are drawn mostly from academic libraries. How well do those collections represent the wider world of fiction? Book historians are often doubtful. (Tuchman and Fortin may have restricted their claim to "*high-culture* novelists" because they anticipated a similar skepticism.) A second problem is that to assign authorial gender to a hundred thousand volumes we had to rely on algorithmic inference, using names recorded in the US Census as a guide.[18] What about ambiguous names or non-European names or pseudonyms or multiple authors?

To address these doubts, I worked with Sabrina Lee to construct a second sample, using independent sources and methods. From 1873 forward, *Publishers Weekly* recorded books published in America. This may not be an exhaustive list of publications, but it definitely includes many things not digitized or preserved in academic libraries. (In fact only 56% of the works of fiction we sampled from *Publishers Weekly* are contained in HathiTrust, and by the late twentieth century the fraction may be closer to 20%.) We manually sampled four years to see whether gender trends in this larger domain would echo trends in academic digital libraries. Since we were manually assigning authors to a gender category, this sample also addressed potential concerns about the accuracy of algorithmic inference based on names. Manual sampling is labor intensive, so our samples are not huge, and the error bars

16. Moretti, *Graphs, Maps, Trees*, 27.

17. Ellen Miller Casey, "Edging Women Out? Reviews of Women Novelists in the *Athenaeum*, 1860–1900," *Victorian Studies* 39 (1996): 154.

18. Inference from personal names was done by Gender-ID.py, created by Bridget Baird and Cameron Blevins, 2014, https://github.com/cblevins/Gender-ID-By-Time.

shown in figure 4.9 leave considerable wiggle room. But it is safe to say that we have found no evidence that the broad trends in HathiTrust are produced merely by library purchasing patterns. Minor fluctuations, such as the suspiciously sharp drop at 1923, for instance, may well be library-specific. But the broad decline in the proportion of fiction written by women is, if anything, even more dramatic in the larger domain sampled by *Publishers Weekly*.

So why did it happen? Tuchman and Fortin offer several good hypotheses about the nineteenth century. First, they emphasize that early-nineteenth-century fiction was dominated by women because novel writing was not yet a high-status career. "After 1840 some men may have become novelists because writing fiction increasingly brought status. Additionally, after 1840 the job conditions of novelists improved."[19] Gentrification stories of this sort are familiar. Talia Schaffer has pointed out that male aesthetes similarly moved in on descriptions of dress and interior décor that had been seen as feminine—until they became too prestigious to leave to women.[20] Secondly, Tuchman and Fortin trace social pressures in literary reviewing, and in the terms of publishers' contracts, that subjected women to increasing disadvantages in the later nineteenth century. (Other scholars have not always agreed: Ellen Miller Casey's close analysis of the *Athenaeum* comes to an opposite conclusion, at least about reviews in one periodical.)[21] Finally, Tuchman and Fortin also acknowledge that intellectual careers other than "novelist" were opening up to women. To fully map this expansion would require many different kinds of social evidence. But if we stick with the evidence of authorship, fiction is one of the few parts of the library where representation of women seems to have declined. If we consider all other categories, collectively, we see an enormous expansion (interrupted by the much briefer sort of pause in the middle of the twentieth century that we might have expected). It is not

19. Tuchman with Fortin, *Edging Women Out*, 9.
20. Talia Schaffer, *The Forgotten Female Aesthetes: Literary Culture in Late-Victorian England* (Charlottesville: University of Virginia Press, 2000), 23–29, 73–87.
21. Casey, "Edging Women Out?," 154–55.

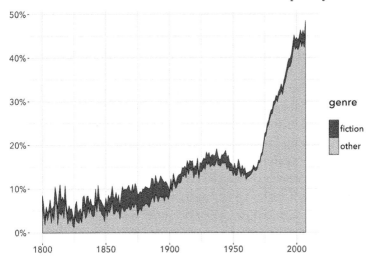

FIGURE 4.10. Books by women as a percentage of all books in HathiTrust. Genres are stacked on top of each other: the top line is cumulative. The category "other" is mostly nonfiction, although it also includes small amounts of poetry and drama.

hard to see how expanding opportunities on the scale shown in figure 4.10 might have lured women away from the novel.

Social causality is never easy to untangle. Tuchman and Fortin, for instance, disagree with Casey about the impact of nineteenth-century reviewing. In this chapter, I won't completely resolve the tension between competing explanations either. But the occupational shifts that Tuchman and Fortin have described—male "gentrification" of the novel and the opening of other careers for women—provide plausible explanations of the changes we see down to, say, 1940. After that point, a different pattern appears: women's participation in fiction and nonfiction move together, down and then (spectacularly) up, possibly in response to the broader fortunes of feminism. From 1940 forward, it appears that authorship of fiction is shaped less by social factors that guided women toward or away from fiction in particular than by broader attitudes toward femininity and work. (The late-twentieth-century rise in women's authorship of fiction would be even more impressive if we included juvenile fiction; that market grows substantially and women are strongly represented in it.)[22]

If this explanation holds, the apparent contradiction between the two halves of this chapter's argument would be no contradiction at all. Because literary historians have a special professional interest in fiction, we may be tempted to view the decline of women's participation in that genre as a barometer of equality generally. If that were true, it would be puzzling to see this index of equality declining in the very period when characters' lives inside fiction were becoming less sharply gendered. But authorship of fiction is actually a poor measure of equality at large. In the early nineteenth century, when the novel was effectively a ghetto for intellectual women, women's dominance of fiction is in part a measure of their segregation. It may not be puzzling at all that increased flexibility of gender roles inside fiction would coincide with a flight into other genres.

Open Questions

The tensions explored in this chapter may tell us something about the relative value of numbers for historical description and for explanation. Descriptively, this chapter has revealed major new patterns. The gender ratio among authors of English-language fiction for adults goes from roughly one to one in the middle of the nineteenth century to roughly three to one in the middle of the twentieth. That is a huge fact about the history of fiction, and it has not been foregrounded in existing surveys of the subject. Different scholars have seen parts of this elephant, so to speak, but it has been difficult to characterize the whole trend confidently. The description provided here is largely new.

On the other hand, the explanations this chapter has provided are not radically novel. Most of the hypotheses I have offered to explain women's declining participation in fiction echo sugges-

---

22. I was prompted to check this detail by Dan Sinykin's presentation "The Conglomerate Era" at the Society for Novel Studies, Ithaca, NY, June 2, 2018.

tions already made by Tuchman and Fortin in *Edging Women Out*. My account may emphasize some hypotheses slightly more than they do and others slightly less. Evidence about the blurring of gender roles, for instance, has tended to nudge this account away from a dark interpretation where the declining prominence of women in fiction might represent actual social backsliding— and toward a story that instead emphasizes growing opportunities in other genres and careers. But both explanations can be found in *Edging Women Out*; neither was original to this chapter.

The same pattern has appeared in several other chapters: this book's real innovations have often been descriptive rather than explanatory. This is odd, because in many familiar situations description precedes explanation. I can describe my symptoms easily, but I need a doctor to diagnose them. A high school student can describe a book's plot, but explaining its historical influences may strain even a professor.

When we back up to look at two hundred years, I would suggest, we are confronting a problem of a basically different kind. On this scale, description is far from easy. In many cases, we have failed to sketch basic trends, because two centuries simply don't fit in a human memory. Quantitative evidence may have to be gathered before description can begin. On the other hand, numbers are not particularly good at unraveling causality on a scale of centuries. There are often many causal factors involved in a single trend; across a long timeline, they may all correlate with each other uninformatively. So causal questions are often better addressed by closely analyzing a few cases, and existing qualitative scholarship has often done that rather well. Nancy Armstrong's account of the gendering of privacy in the early history of the novel is not easy to improve. Neither is Gaye Tuchman's account of the late-nineteenth-century gentrification of fiction. So, although it sounds paradoxical, we should not be surprised to find that quantitative analysis sometimes reveals unexpected patterns—for which we already have several good explanations handy. Qualitative scholarship has often given us a good picture of the causal interaction between variables on a local level without revealing those variables' actual macroscopic behavior across a long timeline.

But there will certainly be cases where quantitative evidence uncovers puzzles that still lack an explanation. This chapter has revealed, for instance, a puzzling tension between the fluidity of gender in fiction and the stability of authorial behavior. Fictive representations of gender seem to be quite volatile. In the nineteenth century femininity is expressed through description of the heart; in the twentieth century, through description of hair. Nineteenth-century men have houses; twentieth-century men have pockets. Moreover, the importance of these differences, collectively, varies greatly across time. On the other hand, there are strangely durable differences between men and women as authors. For two hundred years, men consistently drew more sharply gendered characters than women and consistently underrepresented women in their fictional worlds. This paradox deserves more discussion than I can give it here. But one possible conclusion would be that the structural positions of masculine and feminine identity, vis-à-vis each other, have remained very stable—while the actual content of masculinity and femininity has been entirely mutable.

It is also possible, of course, that this chapter has discovered stable "structural positions" only because it explores gender, for the most part, as a binary opposition. I have presented that binary model as a provisional simplification of public roles, not as a truth about personal identity. But it would be possible to simplify public roles in several different ways. This chapter has implicitly treated changes in the expression of gender as a *convergence* between previously distant positions. But it would also be possible to represent those changes as the *blurring* of a boundary to produce a spectrum or as a *multiplication* of gender identities that made the binary opposition between masculine and feminine increasingly irrelevant to characters' plural roles. Further research could ask which of those models best explains the evidence.

Perspectival questions also deserve more attention than they have received here. Whether we understand gender with Judith

Butler as a performance or (with Linda Martín Alcoff) as a real, although historically constructed, "position one occupies," it is clear that gender is a relational category.[23] It is less a fact about the subject herself than about her relation to a social audience. But there can be, of course, more than one audience. Literary gender might be constructed differently in different genres or in different parts of the literary field. Because predictive models are good at capturing implicit assumptions, they are well suited to teasing out these different perspectives.

For instance, how is femininity represented differently in books by women or by men? I have already mentioned that models trained and tested on books by men consistently find gender easier to predict. But what specific differences are created by authorial perspective? Comparing models reveals (surprise!) that women and men have substantial disagreements about gender. I only have room here for a brief and tentative discussion of this topic. But after training six models on different random samples of characters from 1800 to 1999, I found, for instance, that women writers consistently characterized their feminine characters with words like "spend," "conscience," "busy," and "endeavoured," which books by men had treated as masculine. In books by women, men are often the direct object of the verb "marry"; in books by men, women are. Different sexual identities, obviously, might introduce another kind of perspectival variation here.

There is also a large area of agreement about gender. If we compare the predictions made by different models, those trained on books by one gender correlate at $r = .549$ with those trained on books by the other. But since men and women don't agree with each other quite as much as men do with other random samples of books by men ($r = .666$) or women with other samples of books by women ($r = .594$), it doesn't necessarily seem safe to conclude that we are all talking about the same categories.

---

23. Judith Butler, *Gender Trouble: Feminism and the Subversion of Identity* (New York: Routledge, 1990); Linda Martín Alcoff, *Visible Identities: Race, Gender, and the Self* (Oxford: Oxford University Press, 2006), 148.

In short, quantitative methods could be used not only to trace changes over time but to break the binary categories we began with into four different relationships between observer and observed. Further research on sexuality, nationality, or genre could take us from four perspectives to twelve or twenty. (The men in Zane Grey express gender differently than the men in Daphne Du Maurier's *Rebecca*.)

At some point, of course, predictive models will reach their limits. If we want to discuss specific characters in *Rebecca*, the traditional methods of literary criticism will give us richer descriptive resources. A binary model of gender also has limits, even as a heuristic premise. If we want to bracket gender binaries altogether, we can do so: scholars applying computational methods to social media have used a flexible Butlerian theory of gender to good effect.[24] But if we are interested in teasing out the implicit variations in apparently stable categories, perspectival modeling can be very useful.

---

24. David Bamman, Jacob Eisenstein, and Tyler Schnoebelen, "Gender Identity and Lexical Variation in Social Media," *Journal of Sociolinguistics* 18, no. 2 (2014): 135–60.

5

The Risks of Distant Reading

Like the scientists of *Jurassic Park*, the first four chapters of this book have been "so preoccupied with whether or not they could" use numbers to learn something about literary history, that "they didn't stop to think if they should."[1] In this final chapter, I hope to remedy the oversight by considering the risks of the approach I have taken.

Generally, historical research is less risky than cloning dinosaurs. But applying numbers to the literary past, in particular, remains controversial enough that an analogy to *Jurassic Park* is not absurd. Objections to new methods of analysis run deeper than I have so far acknowledged. Critics claim not that it is impossible to learn anything about literature with numbers but that knowledge of this kind could only be gained by displacing a more appropriately literary mode of insight. The risk is often represented as an ethical temptation or even a slippery slope toward the "death of a discipline."[2]

1. David Koepp, *Jurassic Park*, based on earlier draft by Michael Crichton and Malia Scotch Marmo, December 11, 1992.

2. David Golumbia, "Death of a Discipline," *differences* 25, no. 1 (2014): 156–76; Johanna Drucker, "Humanistic Theory and Digital Scholarship," in *Debates in Digital Humanities*, ed. Matthew K. Gold (Minneapolis: University of Minnesota Press, 2012), 85–95.

I don't imagine that these objections can be brushed aside. Those of us who hold advanced degrees in literary study have invested decades of our lives in a scholarly craft that is also a community. Wariness about an alternative approach to the subject is rarely just a misunderstanding that could be cleared up with a few explanations. Rather, it expresses a set of commitments to existing institutions and social ties. Those commitments change slowly, and an honest discussion of them will need to acknowledge enduring differences of opinion. Discussion of that kind makes more sense in a conclusion than a preface, which is why I have deferred it to the end of this book.

Simply acknowledging that disciplines change slowly may be the most important thing I can say to reassure wary readers. Reassurance has become necessary, I think, because the phrase *digital humanities* encourages scholars to understand new ideas as a wave of technological change, and the pace of technological change can be unsettling. Flat-screen monitors are introduced; in a decade or two everyone is using them. This is possible because technology encapsulates change, literally containing it inside a box. The users of flat-screen monitors can simply switch out their tools, without any need to change their own behavior. Change of this kind is so effortless that it can happen with unreflective speed.

In the first decade of this century, many people hoped that quantitative methods could be introduced to the humanities in an equally painless way. Digital humanists would build tools; everyone else would use them. Scholars might not need to understand all the details inside the box, any more than we have traditionally worried about the innards of a search engine when fishing for sources. Foundations invested millions of dollars trying to support this quick, painless kind of change.[3] But for the most

---

3. For an admirably honest account of one project, see Quinn Dombrowski, "What Ever Happened to Project Bamboo?," *Literary and Linguistic Computing* 29, no. 3 (2014): 326–39. I should acknowledge that infrastructure projects can have many beneficial side effects, even when the infrastructure itself is not widely used. This book may be one of them.

part, it didn't happen. Instead, change has taken place slowly, and mostly through laborious retraining. The reason, I think, is that new methods have turned out to be more consequential than was widely believed a decade ago. Search engines can be encapsulated and treated as tools. But statistical models are not well envisioned as tools: they offer new methods of representing and interpreting the world. Scholars cannot adopt a new mode of interpretation without fully understanding the reasoning it implies.

In acknowledging this, I am admitting that the methods used in this book have the potential to be truly disruptive. "A new way of representing and interpreting the world" would be a significant change in the humanities. But a change this fundamental is also likely to be slow. Statistical models are not going to be on everyone's desk in ten years, like flat-screen monitors. Right now they are used by a tiny fraction of literary scholars (half of 1% would be a generous estimate), and that fraction cannot grow quickly, because statistical modeling requires a semester or two of training not currently offered in literature departments. Other aspects of digital humanities may take the discipline by storm. You can learn to build a website in a week, so many scholars are already building their own websites. But quantitative analysis of large digital libraries requires a massive commitment of time and labor; I would be surprised if even 2% of literary scholars undertook that commitment over the next decade.

Once we distinguish distant reading from the broader topic of digital technology and review the truly marginal position numbers now occupy in the humanities, much debate on this topic becomes laughable. For instance, conversation about distant reading is often shaped by the premise that quantitative methods are displacing (or could soon displace) other critical practices, such as close reading.[4] This concern is wholly hypothetical. Distant readers are a tiny group of scholars, exploring difficult methods

4. Jonathan Freedman, "After Close Reading," *New Rambler* last modified 2015, http://newramblerreview.com/book-reviews/literary-studies/after-close-reading; Barbara Herrnstein Smith, "What Was 'Close Reading'? A Century of Method in Literary Studies," *Minnesota Review* 87, no. 1 (2016): 57–75.

that have as yet no place in the literary curriculum. The only thing they have displaced so far is a small amount of air.

That being said, it remains fair to ask about the long-term implications of new ideas. Literary scholars tend to see their discipline as an isolated enclave in an intellectual landscape dominated by the natural and social sciences. So while numbers play at present only a tiny role in literature departments, even that tiny role awakens understandable concerns. Looking at the positive reception distant reading has received from journalists and in other quarters of the university, scholars find it easy to envision recent quantitative experiments as a small break in a levee that could quickly widen and flood literary studies with external influences.

A great deal of conversation about distant reading is organized by this dark vision of the future. One popular way to allay fears is to reaffirm the autonomy of literature departments by discovering an impenetrable inner wall that numbers could never breach. Arguments of this form often start by admitting that numbers may be useful for some peripheral functions—such as "compiling concordances" or "deciphering Mayan stelae," to borrow two examples from Timothy Brennan. But, the writer will continue, an inherent flaw in numeric representation makes numbers unfit for the core purposes of literary study ("the interpretive problems . . . that have long stumped critics.")[5] Often it turns out that numbers can never illuminate individual works of literature or that they are incapable of grappling with subjective and perspectival evidence.[6]

In this chapter, I am likewise trying to measure the risks of distant reading, in order to reassure a worried discipline. Numbers can be valuable, especially for large historical questions. But I doubt they will ever exclude, or even significantly displace, other approaches to literature. However, I can hardly express this reassurance by affirming the solidity of a wall that separates quantitative reasoning from interpretation or from the study of individual texts. I have already spent most of this book poking holes in that

5. Timothy Brennan, "The Digital Humanities Bust," *Chronicle of Higher Education*, October 20, 2017.

6. Both arguments are implied in Johanna Drucker, "Why Distant Reading Isn't," *PMLA* 132, no. 3 (2017): 628–35.

imagined wall. While it is true that numbers are mostly useful at large scales of analysis, for instance, I have stressed that different scales of description are closely connected. In chapter 2, a model trained on hundreds of books also illuminated a single novel by identifying a single paragraph that exemplified its divergence from earlier works of science fiction. Subjective evidence about genre, gender, and literary quality has also been central to my argument, which has steadily resisted the notion that a firm boundary can be drawn between measurement and interpretation.

So instead of defending literary studies negatively—by proving that numbers are unable to address our questions—I will have to take a positive approach. The reason literary scholars are unlikely to use math in every article is simply that literary scholarship already excels at its own mission. We probably *could* use computational analysis to assist every close reading. It wouldn't be epistemically impossible or ethically perilous to do so. It's just that we can usually do a better (more vivid, more concise) job on our own. Instead of inventing a stretched story about the dangers of quantification, in other words, I propose to limit the authority of numbers in the humanities by remembering to appreciate some things we already do well. A list of that kind could become long, because there are many things literary scholars do well. But in the context of this discussion it is particularly worth recalling that the strengths of literary criticism have typically echoed the strengths of the literary works we discuss. One risk of distant reading is that we might forget the connection.

The Risk of Forgetting Pleasure

One has to be careful not to generalize too hastily here, because "literature" is a fluid concept, and the dominant contemporary sense of the word is not much more than a hundred years old.[7]

7. It is commonly said that the modern concept of literature takes shape in the eighteenth century, but as Anders Pettersson points out, the concept continues to narrow substantially in the nineteenth century. Anders Pettersson, "Introduction: Concepts of Literature and Transcultural Literary History," in *Literary History: Towards a Global Perspective*, ed. Gunilla Lindberg-Wada (Berlin: Walter de Gruyter, 2006), 1:1–35.

Seventeenth- and eighteenth-century writers would be puzzled by our assumption that literature inevitably takes sides with imagination and against reason, with the individual quirk and against the aggregate trend. But it is fairly safe to observe that people have cared about literary history because they enjoy novels, plays, and poems. A version of literary history that didn't help readers understand the pleasure of reading would have little reason to exist. Moreover, histories of literary enjoyment become more interesting if they are enlivened by flickers of resonance between the spirit of the description and the spirit of the works described. Resonance with literary enjoyment doesn't necessarily rule out math: numbers can create a wide variety of effects, from suspense to sublimity. But writers who want to remind readers of enjoyment are probably wise to avoid the fixed expository formulas that prevail in quantitative social science (methods, results, conclusions).

The boundary between the humanities and social sciences is not often described this bluntly. Suggesting that literary scholarship is distinguished from (say) linguistics by its resonance with pleasure seems rude to social scientists. At the same time it wounds the dignity of humanists, by hinting that we are at some level entertainers. (Like most intellectuals, we would prefer to imagine that we are communing with Truth and Critique.) So while literary scholars widely agree that their discipline is divided from social science by some underlying purpose of literature itself, we rarely identify simple enjoyment as the purpose at stake. Instead, we invent theories about a form of knowledge that only literary critics have access to—because we alone attend to the subtleties of language or the constitutive paradoxes of thought or the ethical consequences of human diversity. But of course linguists, psychologists, and sociologists attend to those things as well.

Literary scholars do have a special form of knowledge. But the candid way to define its distinctiveness is to say that we have the privilege of focusing on things that are interesting or enjoyable. We often abbreviate debate on intricate questions by using interpretive judgment to foreground patterns readers are likely to care about. This privilege of selective emphasis can be abused, producing blind spots. In fact, the thesis of this book is that hasty assumptions about narrative interest have focused literary history too narrowly on the scale of the individual author or generation, leading us to ignore spectacular longer-term trends. But although errors of that scope are possible, narrative interest is still vital for a subject like literature, which stops mattering if readers stop caring about it. I hope it is clear, at this point, that literary historians do need computational methods to grasp narrative arcs that would otherwise be hidden by their sheer length. But we can never afford to let the sophistication of our methods upstage the human interest of our subject. That emphasis might be tolerable in economics, but it would be fatal to the pleasures that make literature worth writing about. Distant readers will need to practice an unobtrusive kind of quantitative rigor—scrupulous and patient with details but partly deferred to appendixes so the literary subject itself can take center stage.

To be fair, distant reading is hardly the only branch of literary history to run a risk of dryness lately. Rita Felski suggests that the ascendance of "critique" as a goal may have led the discipline to forget enjoyment. Joseph North argues that literary historicism, as far back as the 1980s, lost touch with the cultivation of sensibility that gave criticism a social purpose.[8] These persuasive observations have a tendency to devolve into debates about blame that I don't intend to explore here. Disciplinary changes are not always the consequence of any fateful mistake. A shift from aesthetic appreciation to historicism and moralism is exactly what we might expect to see, for instance, if novel reading itself were slowly becoming less central to popular culture and more closely associated with classrooms. That sentence is phrased subjunctively because I don't know that it explains recent trends. I am just observing that we have no reason yet to assume that anyone

8. Rita Felski, *The Limits of Critique* (Chicago: University of Chicago Press, 2015); North, *Literary Criticism*.

is to blame for those trends. In any event, the way to make literary history less dry and moralistic is not to argue moralistically about the source of dryness.

So I am not going to suggest that I can diagnose all the ailments of literary study or that distant reading alone is the cure. I do want to argue that distant reading can help rather than hurt. Unreflectively turning literary scholarship into social science would be a bad idea. Quantitative arguments can bog down in finicky details, and detailism would aggravate a recent tendency to separate literary history from pleasure. But detailism is not inevitable. At its best, distant reading pushes in the other direction, adding a new liveliness and sweep to historical inquiry. Big questions are inherently intriguing, and the best distant readers have also been thoughtful about expository form. The Stanford Literary Lab pamphlets, for instance, use the experimental structure of quantitative inquiry to generate suspense but combine that experimental plot line with sensitive close readings of individual works. In short, math can never release literary critics from their obligation to be interesting. But a careful writer can connect math to literary pleasure in interesting ways. In fact, if hubris is interesting, I suspect distant readers will more than do their part. The notion that distant reading expresses a "new modesty in literary criticism" is the most amusing thing ever written about it.[9]

But I am only willing to separate literary history from social science by bluntly emphasizing literary interest and enjoyment. Scholars who try to draw a more idealized boundary between methodologies often end up universalizing narrower and more tendentious claims about the purpose of literature. One such claim, popular for the last century or so, presents literature as a mode of knowledge that resists generalization in order to acknowledge the specificity of lived experience. In the middle of the twentieth century, this theory became central to the move-

9. Jeffrey Williams, "The New Modesty in Literary Criticism," *Chronicle of Higher Education*, January 5, 2015, http://www.chronicle.com/article/The-New-Modesty-in-Literary/150993.

ment that John Crowe Ransom dubbed the New Criticism. For Ransom, poetry is a "more 'realistic' kind of cognition" than science because it acknowledges the limits of generalization: "The technical structures under which the scientists try to grasp the world . . . make no provision for the local detail which goes with actual body."[10] Midcentury poets celebrated their own vocation in a similar way. W. H. Auden's "In Praise of Limestone" gave the ideal of particularity an appropriately concrete expression, contrasting the lure of "infinite" and "permanent" spaces to a human-sized and "private" landscape:

> hear the springs
> That spurt out everywhere with a chuckle,
> Each filling a private pool for its fish and carving
> Its own little ravine whose cliffs entertain
> The butterfly and the lizard; examine this region
> Of short distances and definite places.[11]

In attacking C. P. Snow, F. R. Leavis advanced a more dogmatic version of the ideal of particularity: "Only in living individuals is life there, and individual lives cannot be aggregated or equated or dealt with quantitatively in any way."[12]

This ideal has many different forms. Sometimes writers emphasize personal individuality, sometimes the concreteness of sense experience, sometimes the impossibility of measurement and comparison. But in one form or another, a contrast between generalization and particularity has remained central to literary critics' sense of their mission for a century. If it was temporarily challenged by Marxism and structuralism, the ideal of particularity reasserted its authority in postmodern celebration of local knowledge and—perhaps most influentially—in the form of the New Historicist anecdote. As Stephen Greenblatt and Catherine

10. John Crowe Ransom, *The New Criticism* (Norfolk, CT: New Directions, 1941), 43.
11. W. H. Auden, "In Praise of Limestone," *Collected Shorter Poems 1927–1957* (1948; New York: Random House, 1964), 238–39.
12. F. R. Leavis, *Two Cultures? The Significance of C. P. Snow* (London: Chatto and Windus, 1962), 20.

Gallagher explain, "The miniature completeness of the anecdote necessarily interrupts the continuous flow of larger histories." Like Ransom's "local details" that exceed the "technical structures" trying to grasp them, the anecdote exceeds its ostensibly illustrative function, and thereby "divulges a different reality, which is behind or beside the narrative surface and composed of things that historians cannot assimilate into typicality or coherent significance." For Gallagher and Greenblatt, the incommensurable specificity of the anecdote links criticism both to the realist novel and to the anthropology of Clifford Geertz, while separating it from the "generalizable typicality" of the "Big Stories" told by Marxist or Annaliste historians.[13]

A sense that critics are sworn to resist "generalizable typicality" also lies, of course, at the root of many objections to distant reading. I think this impulse springs from a range of motives—some quite legitimate, others dubious. One important motive has been a desire for disciplinary autonomy. As my quotations from Ransom, Leavis, Gallagher, and Greenblatt make clear, championing incommensurable particulars has often given literary scholars a way to declare independence from other researchers, whether historians or scientists. This impulse to hold other disciplines at arm's length has been central to recent methodological debate, and I don't expect to persuade every reader here. But personally, I think it is a mistake to let contemporary academic boundaries confine our definition of literature. I have already admitted that literary scholars feel besieged by other forms of knowledge. But self-defense is a raison d'état that too quickly justifies incuriosity and seals a discipline off from the world. Many of the writers we study refused to separate literature so crisply from other human pursuits. "No man is an island," wrote John Donne, in a "Medita-

---

13. Catherine Gallagher and Stephen Greenblatt, *Practicing New Historicism* (Chicago: University of Chicago Press, 2000), 50–51. For a more skeptical take on this aspect of New Historicism, see Alan Liu, "Local Transcendence: Cultural Criticism, Postmodernism, and the Romanticism of Detail," *Representations* 32 (1990): 75–113. For a longer historical perspective, David Simpson, *The Academic Postmodern and the Rule of Literature: A Report on Half-Knowledge* (Chicago: University of Chicago Press, 1995).

tion" that was neither exactly a prose poem nor exactly a sermon. "Every man is a piece of the continent, a part of the main."[14]

However, leaving the contested question of disciplinary autonomy to one side, I would acknowledge in any case that the pleasures of particularity are also rooted deeply and genuinely in modern literature itself—in self-consciously concrete poetry like Auden's and in the random-seeming details of the realist novel. These pleasures are legitimately dear to critics, both in themselves and because they create openings for a characteristically modern form of critical virtuosity. Willfully concrete writing puts the critic in the position of an oracular mediator, able to translate fragmentary sense impressions into something more communal. ("The taste of this cookie dipped in tea describes not just the narrator's own past—but something about memory generally, or modernism generally, or the commodity form generally.") That dazzling leap across scales of description, connecting an instant of personal experience to collective historical time, is one of the distinctive achievements of modern criticism.[15] It would be tragic if distant readers were required to renounce it.

Fortunately, we are not. I have suggested that literary historians need numbers and statistical models to correct a blind spot in their understanding of the past. But correcting a blind spot doesn't require us to renounce other forms of knowledge. In writing this book, I have consciously sought to work with the strengths of post-Romantic literature, anchoring models of century-spanning change in tiny moments of lived experience—from the insistence on color that shapes a conversation between two lovers in *The Invaders* to the oddly gendered grinning and chuckling of Raymond Chandler's brutal men. I do want to point out, however, that the brief and theatrically arbitrary moments of experience I have used to anchor this narrative are illustrations of a distinctly modern kind. Before Romanticism, poetry often aimed for the

14. John Donne, *Devotions upon Emergent Occasions* (Ann Arbor: University of Michigan Press, 1959), 108.
15. For more on this pleasure, see Sharon Marcus, "Erich Auerbach's *Mimesis* and the Value of Scale," *MLQ* 77 no. 3 (2016): 297–319.

"generalizable typicality" that Gallagher and Greenblatt disdain. Before the novel, narrative often traded in general types as well. So I don't draw any normative lesson from this book's scattered moments of concrete specificity. I didn't write those passages because close and distant scales of analysis must always be mixed in a specific ratio. I wrote them merely because a history of post-Romantic writing will be more entertaining if it resonates with post-Romantic pleasures.

But that pleasurable resonance with the object of inquiry needn't prevent us from stepping back to distant-read the pleasures themselves. In the previous paragraph, I loosely described concrete specificity as a "specifically modern" and "post-Romantic" pleasure. But a reader who has skimmed the earlier chapters of this book will be able to date the pleasures of concreteness in a richer, less binary way, because this whole book has traced the gradual emergence of concreteness as a literary ideal.

Having measured the curve of that emergence, we don't have to bog down in a semantic debate about the precise degree of credit that should go to a vaguely defined Romantic dividing line. We can say confidently that insistence on concrete detail is not a timeless feature of fiction and poetry (as John Crowe Ransom maintained) but a feature that rose to prominence across the past 240 years (see figure 1.2). Going a little further, we can observe that emphasis on concrete detail was not a change that affected modern writing in general. It was a shift restricted to literary genres and was one of the primary ways they diverged from nonfiction over the past three centuries. Moreover, this was not an inchoate, drifting trend—a mere line on a graph. It was also a coherent social practice. We can define it synchronically by studying the preferences of nineteenth-century reviewers, who consistently favored poems that used the first-person singular and stories that emphasized concrete description, while tending to ignore stories and poems that relied on social generalization.

Critics of distant reading often suggest that measuring social trends is at odds with the pleasure of literature itself. "Literature," as the phrase goes, "is not data."[16] More careful critics, like Caroline Levine, say more specifically that generalizing about aggregates is in tension with relatively *recent* literary forms—for instance, with the Victorian realist novel, which "seems to go out of its way to avoid . . . the use of numbers." Precision on this historical point makes a difference. Numbers are common enough in *Robinson Crusoe*, after all, and even in *Twenty Thousand Leagues Under the Sea*. The panoramas opened up by large numbers can incite the speculative imagination. But nineteenth-century realists like Charles Dickens and George Eliot did develop a habit of suggesting social scale only indirectly, through close-up depiction of a few cases that stand in for "uncountable particulars."[17] A candid distant reader needs to acknowledge the force of this critique: over the last two centuries, high literary culture has genuinely committed itself to uncountable particularity. But it follows that, by tracing the rise of this literary ideal, distant readers can help explain some of the resistance to distant reading.

I don't mean that we can explain resistance away. The jujitsu that uses a literary theory to dismiss resistance to the theory itself may be familiar to readers of Paul de Man.[18] But the interpretive practices of distant readers don't have the dissolving power of De Man's abstractions. Instead of reducing resistance to a symptom of an underlying paradox, we can at most describe it as the result of a two-century trend. This step toward self-understanding may perhaps give us some reflective distance from presentist assumptions. But characterizing the pleasure of literary concreteness as the result of a contingent historical process will not, I hope, dispel the pleasure itself. Resistance to social abstraction remains a living fact of contemporary literary culture, and literary

---

16. Stephen Marche, "Literature Is Not Data: Against Digital Humanities," *Los Angeles Review of Books*, October 8, 2012, https://lareviewofbooks.org/article/literature-is-not-data-against-digital-humanities/.

17. Caroline Levine, "The Enormity Effect: Realist Fiction, Literary Studies, and the Refusal to Count," *Genre* 50, no. 1 (2017): 60, 69.

18. Paul de Man, "The Resistance to Theory," *Yale French Studies* 63 (1982): 3–20.

historians who want to generalize about the past (whether quantitatively or qualitatively) must acknowledge that their goals are partly in tension with contemporary literary pleasures.

However, this is not to say that the literature of all eras is hostile to generalization or that the humanities are permanently divided from the social sciences by a refusal to generalize. A scholar who combines close readings with mathematical models certainly does transgress contemporary academic boundaries. But I see no reason to believe that this transgression breaks any permanent law. On the contrary, we have good reason to think that the expansion of scale permitted by mathematics will help us address a presentist blind spot created by literature's contemporary association with individuality and particularity.

Enjoyment, on the other hand, comes pretty close to a permanent law of literary culture. So the real challenge to large-scale literary analysis is not epistemic or ethical but aesthetic: it is simply hard to write with sweep and verve about thousands of books. Obstacles come from several directions. Colleagues from the sciences will urge a writer to add more statistical tests. Formalist critics will ask for more close readings. Book historians will ask for a bibliography that separates different editions. There is no contradiction in doing all of the above, except that at some point arguments get weighed down by detail and lose the energy that makes readers care about literary criticism. So, to return to the title of this chapter: normative arguments about distant reading may have distracted us from the most urgent risk of this project, which is rhetorical difficulty. Interdisciplinary argument on this scale requires careful attention to a mass of detail; at the same time, it needs to establish what I've called "a pleasurable resonance" with the literature it is discussing. That delicate balance can fail in many ways.

The Risk of Preoccupation with Technology

A second risk of distant reading is the danger of conflating new interpretive methods with new technologies. In this volume,

I have represented distant reading as a mode of interpretation rather than a computing technology. I have also emphasized its twentieth-century roots, describing the regression models in *Edging Women Out*, for instance, as precursors.[19] Although I do use computers to create the models described in this book, I haven't spent a lot of time talking about digital technology. But in the wider world, distant reading is often understood as a sort of technical wizardry recently invented in Silicon Valley. Critics of the method sometimes assert that it is elitist because "servers powerful enough to process big data can only be located in a highly select number of well-endowed institutions."[20] This kind of fearmongering is the flip side of technophilic hype; both are wildly exaggerated. Managing a whole digital library, like Hathi-Trust, is admittedly a big task. But specific research questions usually engage a small part of the library. Most of the analysis in this book can be done on a desktop, although some of the programs might take an afternoon to run. Nothing discussed here required computing power that is available only at a few institutions.

Sometimes, scholars using computational methods can themselves become too hypnotized by the physical embodiment of these methods in computers. Several digital humanists have rightly warned the field against the fantasy that delegating observation to a machine would somehow increase the objectivity of results.[21] This fantasy—which Lorraine Daston and Peter Galison have called "mechanical objectivity"—may be evoked especially by unsupervised learning algorithms (such as clustering and topic modeling) that seem to discover patterns in the archive

19. Tuchman with Fortin, *Edging Women Out*, 231–40.

20. Moira Weigel, "Graphs and Legends," *Nation*, May 12, 2015, https://www.thenation.com/article/graphs-and-legends/.

21. See Bernhard Rieder and Theo Röhle, "Digital Methods: Five Challenges," in *Understanding Digital Humanities*, ed. David M. Berry (Basingstoke: Palgrave, 2012), 67–84. Similar questions are raised by Alan Liu, "The Meaning of the Digital Humanities," *PMLA* 128, no. 2 (2013): 409–23; Ryan Cordell, "Objectivity and Distant Reading," last modified June 8, 2017, http://ryancordell.org/research/objectivity-1/.

without human prompting.[22] In reality, algorithms are designed by human beings and explicitly encode human assumptions. Contemporary computer science is quite lucid on this topic and has become insistent about representing assumptions as Bayesian priors—initial states of belief that will be updated by subsequent analysis. But the humanists who take up a method like topic modeling are not necessarily immersed in these habits of thought. They may give lip service to the notion that algorithms encode subjective assumptions, while still feeling that unsupervised algorithms are somehow more impressive than other forms of analysis, because they generate meaning more spontaneously.

In the long run, this misunderstanding can be cleared up if humanists and scientists acquire a basic understanding of each other's methods, based on contemporary realities rather than caricatures of nineteenth-century Romanticism and positivism. Mutual understanding would lead us away from the fantasy that objectivity and subjectivity represent firmly distinct alternatives and toward a more flexible conversation about human attempts to understand the world by modeling it.[23] Unsupervised learning algorithms have a valid place in that conversation. But in the short run, since humanists are still unfamiliar with statistical models, I felt it was important for this book to indicate clearly that the value of modeling has nothing to do with delegating interpretation to a machine. So unsupervised algorithms don't appear in this book. Instead, I have made a point of emphasizing the grounded character of supervised algorithms—which explicitly acknowledge the circularity of historical interpretation, describing human artifacts only in relation to other artifacts characterized by humans.

But technological fetishism is not narrowly focused on any particular category of algorithm; it can take many forms. Network diagrams, for instance, have a contemporary prestige that

22. Lorraine Daston and Peter Galison, *Objectivity* (New York: Zone, 2010), 42–44.

23. So, "All Models Are Wrong"; Gelman and Hennig, "Beyond Subjective and Objective in Statistics."

often outweighs their actual usefulness. The mysterious attraction of these diagrams owes something to the mathematical sublime and something to the way they echo the emergent authority of the internet.[24] Intellectuals need to keep a wry eye on fashions of this kind. Because digital technology is so saturated with hype and fear, this book uses the word *digital* itself very sparingly. It appears in my subtitle, admittedly, because topics have to be described in familiar terms when an author first greets a reader. But in the text of this book I have usually written instead about statistics, social science, long timelines, or even Arabic numerals. None of those things are new. But they are relatively new in literary history, and we still have much to learn from them.

   If critics of distant reading would likewise acknowledge that the technologies at stake often date back to the middle of the twentieth century, conversation on this topic could move beyond technophilia and -phobia. Few of the ideas currently transforming literary history are really dependent on "big data," for instance. But the phrase has become indispensable for critics of quantitative methods in the humanities, because it implicitly characterizes any use of numbers as a recent fashion, originating in Silicon Valley, and linked in an unspecified way to mass surveillance. I don't think that rhetoric does much to advance mutual understanding.

   In the twenty-first century, the social consequences of digital technology definitely need discussion. The internet has transformed our politics; machine learning is beginning to transform economic life; both changes will have profound consequences. But to argue about technological changes, we need to understand the ideas they rest on, which are less esoteric than commercial hype and defensive anti-intellectualism have led us to believe. Statistical models, for instance, are not recent inventions. It is true that machine learning has made it easier to apply statistical models to unstructured text, but the intellectual advance in-

---

24. For a fuller history of the "network sublime," see Patrick Jagoda, *Network Aesthetics* (Chicago: University of Chicago Press, 2016).

volved there is not mysterious. A short explanation: the strategic addition of blurriness to models makes it possible to avoid the false precision that would otherwise come with complex textual evidence. (I give a longer explanation and suggestions for further reading in appendix B.) The models produced by machine learning do not have to be black boxes. They can be complex but transparent moves in an interpretive argument, and they deserve to be engaged or critiqued as arguments, not hyped or smeared by association with the Bay Area.

In any case, I have worked very hard to separate badly framed controversies about technology from the historical and interpretive questions posed in this book. Instead of presenting distant reading as a conversation about the word *data*, for instance, I have tried to foreground a trio of older words that better characterize the ideas at issue here. First, I have emphasized the premise that historical inquiry can be structured as an *experiment*. To be sure, historians who want to use this word will have to stretch it beyond its ordinary association with beakers and prisms. We cannot intervene in the past and then ask whether it changed as our hypothesis predicted. But this is a problem shared by geologists and astronomers. Distant reading is a historical science, and it will need something like Carol Cleland's definition of scientific method, which embraces not only future-oriented interventions but any systematic test that seeks "to protect the hypothesis from misleading confirmations."[25] We can minimize misleading confirmations, for instance, by testing a hypothesis against a *sample* of texts, defined in advance in order to limit the researcher's freedom to support a predetermined thesis. Finally, I have suggested that historical experiments will often describe samples of the cultural past by testing *models*, or simplified representations of the relations between different concepts. This book relies especially

25. Carol E. Cleland, "Historical Science, Experimental Science, and the Scientific Method," *Geology* 29, no. 11 (2001): 988. My language here closely echoes my own discussion of this issue in "A Genealogy of Distant Reading," *Digital Humanities Quarterly* 11, no. 2 (2017): paragraph 22, http://www.digitalhumanities.org/dhq/vol/11/2/000317/000317.html#p22.

on statistical models: simplified probabilistic relations between variables.

Experiments, samples, models. These are not new technologies; they are the central concepts of twentieth-century social science. So, to frame a fair critique of distant reading, one might ask whether it simply moves further toward social science than most literary scholars are willing to go.

The Missing Curricular Foundation

In particular, one urgent pragmatic question is whether the training required for this project can fit into the curricular structure of a literature department. If not, then the project needs to go elsewhere. Intellectually, literary sociology may shade into book history, and book history may shade into the history of literary form. But practically, we have to decide where to divide departments and majors.

This pragmatic problem—that distant reading may simply exceed the flexibility of our disciplinary institutions—is the last risk I want to discuss in this chapter. It is unfortunately the hardest of the three to evade. The aesthetic risks of distant reading can be minimized by concise, vivid writing. The danger of conflation with technology can be addressed by ignoring hype and emphasizing intellectual foundations. But creating a curriculum to prepare students as distant readers will require the work of many hands over several decades. To pose meaningful questions, researchers in this field need a deep understanding of literary history in at least one national context. But they also need a good understanding of statistics and a bit of hands-on programming experience. Exposure to linguistics or sociology can be helpful; so can a basic understanding of machine learning. It is not impossible to cover this range of topics in six years, but right now very few graduate programs guide students across the terrain.

The first four chapters of this book have argued that open questions about literary history above the scale of a single period constitute a huge intellectual opportunity. I feel some confidence that opportunities on that scale don't go unexplored for long in modern universities. But building disciplinary institutions that can explore them remains a difficult task, and it is not entirely clear who will take it on. When I explained the challenges of teaching quantitative analysis in literature departments at a workshop convened by the National Academies of Science, a representative from Google (Peter Norvig) asked whether it might not be easier simply to teach some literary history to graduate students in information science. I'm afraid it was a perceptive remark. Digital libraries are open to everyone. It is entirely possible that departments of sociology, communications, and information science will be better positioned to explore them than departments of English or French.

Personally, I would regret that outcome. I would like to see literary critics remain central to the large-scale exploration of literary history. People who have been trained to care about historical differences tend to cast a more interesting light on the past than people who care mainly about new methods. On the other hand, I have to acknowledge that literature is a shared human legacy. It is not the property of a single discipline. Writers who assume an audience entirely composed of literature professors often frame questions about distant reading as an intradisciplinary debate. Should departments of literature open their gates to the social sciences, or could the discipline defend literature more effectively by restricting itself to familiar methods? If I were to venture a guess about that question, I would say that disciplines rarely grow stronger by limiting their interaction with the rest of the world. But more fundamentally, I think the question is based on a false premise: it assumes that the history of literature is securely contained in literature departments. Academic disciplines are very durable institutions, but in the long run they are ancillary means to the end of human self-understanding. So instead of addressing a single discipline, this book has tried to address a broader audience of people who want to understand the human past. Some readers may be sociologists or librarians or computer programmers; quantitative inquiry about literary culture can be at home in all of those places.

If we literary scholars also want to make a home for large-scale quantitative research in our departments, we will need to create a curricular path for it. The path doesn't need to be daunting. Students don't need to be polymaths. They just need a semester of statistics and some programming experience (and perhaps a course in social science) added to their training in literary history. This program of study could easily become an optional concentration at the graduate level, culminating perhaps in a capstone course that fuses quantitative methods with historical inquiry. A concentration of that kind could be widely accessible. On the other hand, I do think a curriculum for distant readers should guard against a couple of tempting shortcuts. One is the notion that quantitative methods can simply be delegated to collaborators from other disciplines. As mentioned in my acknowledgments, parts of this book are deeply indebted to collaboration, because the task was too much for one pair of hands. But researchers using quantitative methods have to be able to stand behind their own statistical reasoning. Social scientists don't outsource statistics, and there is no reason for humanists to do so either.

The other shortcut I would warn against is even more tempting: it involves folding distant reading into the cloudier topic of digital humanities. "DH" is a fascinating concept, defined in many different ways. But I understand it less as a distinct field than as a "tactical term," to borrow Matthew Kirschenbaum's phrase.[26] The concept of digital humanities has often provided a tactful collective name for projects that were controversial if advertised separately. "New media studies" was too specifically contemporary. "Distant reading" was too controversially quantitative. But everyone used computers in one way or another, so a wide range of students and faculty in the humanities could unite around a loosely digital common denominator. *Digital humanities* opened up a possibility of change, while remaining strategi-

26. Matthew G. Kirschenbaum, "Digital Humanities As/Is a Tactical Term," in *Debates in Digital Humanities*, ed. Matthew K. Gold (Minneapolis: University of Minnesota Press, 2012), 415–28.

cally vague about the change envisioned. This strategy has been successful in many ways: it got institutional initiatives off the ground and created a lively, inclusive community. But it hasn't done much to define a program of study, and the program it defines doesn't always align well with distant reading.

To the extent that *digital humanities* is defined at all, it is defined by the common denominator of digital technology. But as I have emphasized, technology is not the best frame for distant reading: in fact, phrases like *big data* can be actively damaging. The newness of technological vocabulary also seems to make humanists forget that they could learn from other disciplines and instead imagine that they have to reinvent everything from scratch. Instead of encouraging students to take statistics, for instance, digital humanists tend to organize workshops on the nature of data in the humanities. Those events can be valuable. But I think students would usually learn even more by getting out and breathing the air of an unfamiliar discipline. Finally, framing every conversation as a question about technology also tends to obscure the deep roots of this project in literary study itself. Raymond Williams was already grappling with a *longue durée* in the 1960s; Janice Radway was already structuring literary inquiry as a quantitative experiment in the 1980s.[27] Those writers are still good models for students to imitate—much better models, for instance, than a dizzyingly sublime network graph.

So, to sum up the last of the three risks this chapter has explored, distant reading confronts an interesting set of institutional challenges. It has deep roots in literary history that it cannot afford to forget. On the other hand, many of the most fruitful paths for future exploration require methods not yet taught in literature departments. The usual solution to this dilemma is a flexible, multidisciplinary rubric called digital humanities. But the concept of digital humanities can be too diffuse, or too focused on technology, to foster the kind of preparation distant readers

---

27. Raymond Williams, *The Long Revolution* (1961; Harmondsworth: Penguin 1984); Radway, *Reading the Romance.*

need. Different institutions will probably address this challenge in different ways; I don't have a perfect solution to offer. In fact, I have been acknowledging throughout this chapter that distant reading is a difficult project. Since literary study sometimes imagines itself as a dialectical succession of dominant trends (New Criticism, poststructuralism, New Historicism), we may expect important initiatives either to fail outright or to sweep quickly across the discipline. But interdisciplinary initiatives can be durable and important without rapidly transforming any of the disciplines they touch. Literary scholars tend to be adventurous; I think we will find large historical patterns too interesting to resist exploring them. But building a curricular pipeline to support large-scale quantitative research is another matter. Curricular institutions change slowly even when change is uncontroversial. In this case, literature departments would have to give mathematics a role in the curriculum. The role envisioned may be small, but for a discipline that has long defined itself around Levine's "uncountable particulars," the idea that numbers belong in the literary curriculum at all will evoke fierce controversy. Also, candidly, English majors are not exactly clamoring for a required course in statistics. A discipline concerned about declining enrollment may rightly suspect that other innovations—for instance game studies—would have wider appeal.

So I suspect distant reading will follow the trajectory of the sociology of literature—a field that has attracted senior scholars from several disciplines and produced a series of influential books across sixty-odd years without ever acquiring a secure home in the undergraduate literature major.[28] I hope it will be possible for graduate students to get training in distant reading, but at many institutions, they may have to cobble together courses from several departments.

28. At least since Robert Escarpit, *Sociologie de la littérature* (Paris: Presses Universitaires de France, 1958). James F. English has in fact suggested that distant reading is a recent, peculiarly controversial incarnation of the sociology of literature. English, "Everywhere and Nowhere."

A Final Risk: Addiction to Distant Reading

This chapter has been organized around a series of risks and obstacles. But I nevertheless expect to see many more books like this one. The risks of this project are more than matched by its rewards.

I was drawn to quantitative literary history as a graduate student in the 1990s, before digital libraries even existed to support the enterprise. Soon after the libraries were created, I plunged in and have never looked back. The reason is simple: the work is addictive. Like all historical research, it has the circular suspense of a detective story. Each clue fosters a new suspicion, which in turn uncovers a new clue. But distant reading adds a further pleasure that I never experienced as intensely in other forms of scholarship: the possibility of a vertiginous twist ending. At the start of a distant reading project, my attention is necessarily focused on the individual texts I am selecting for a sample. But when things come together at the end, there is often a dizzying change of perspective, as a larger pattern belatedly becomes visible. I may have to reframe my initial question, which not uncommonly produces a second surprise. The effect resembles the vertigo at the end of certain thriller plots, when the assumptions governing a fictional universe are shaken, narrators are revealed as unreliable, and the meanings of earlier events are retrospectively revised. Once a researcher gets addicted to this feeling of sudden recognition, it is hard to stop asking questions, even if each new twist demands another month of detail work.

Although the shifts of scale in distant reading may intensify the vertigo, I think these pleasures are basically congruent with the satisfaction of all humanistic research. At bottom, the plot of this thriller is about learning to doubt one's own perspective. Sometimes the twists in the story are provided by statistical analysis (which excels, for instance, at measuring uncertainty and distinguishing signal from noise). Sometimes the twists are provided by humanistic theory (which excels at fostering materialist suspicion about the real forces driving the apparent plot). These interpretive traditions are often presented as incompatible. But when both traditions are genuinely understood, I believe there is no conflict between them. On the contrary, they dovetail to produce a more interesting and perplexing world.

The questions that fuel this mode of inquiry will not soon be exhausted. At the moment, distant reading may look like a marginal project, addressing questions of an unusual kind for literary scholars. This book, for instance, has focused on very large-scale phenomena—trends that produced massive changes across two- and three-hundred-year timelines. That choice of subject could easily give the impression that numbers are only useful for the very biggest and coarsest questions about the past. If so, their value for other scholars might be limited. But not all the limitations of this book are inherent to quantitative method. It is true that numbers tend to become more useful at large scales of inquiry. But this book's emphasis on the *very* largest historical patterns has been shaped by the temporary rhetorical obstacles that confront a controversial innovation.

Throughout this project, I have been acutely conscious of addressing a field that still doubts numbers can reveal anything of significance about literature. In a conversation shaped by that assumption, arguments that adjust our interpretation of local historical details tend to be brushed aside with impatience. "Didn't we already know that?" skeptics often respond. "Or couldn't we have learned it in some other way, without numbers?" The answer may be debatable, but it is hard to persuade skeptics by debating hypotheticals. So I have chosen to begin with the biggest trends, where it is fairly clear that someone would already have described the pattern if it had been a pattern the unaided eye could discern. To convince humanists, I also felt that my evidence had to greatly exceed ordinary social-scientific thresholds. It was necessary, but never sufficient, for results to be statistically significant. Effects had to be obvious to the eye once graphed—things like a shift from a one-to-one gender ratio among novelists in the mid-nineteenth century to a three-to-one ratio in the mid-twentieth.

If literary historians are capable of missing a change of that magnitude, then we have undoubtedly also missed a host of less obvious but equally important stories. It is easy to see where some of those stories lie. In the course of writing this book, I have deliberately trimmed many threads of inquiry that would have led toward more complicated methods or sparser sources of evidence. I have tended to neglect the period before 1800, for instance, because data are harder to gather there. I restricted this book mostly to Anglo-American literature (plus a scattering of authors in translation), but Hoyt Long and Richard Jean So have already shown that the same methods can be used to trace histories that cross linguistic boundaries.[29] To avoid burying readers under technical details, I focused mostly on a single computational strategy: predictive modeling. I believe predictive models offer a perspectival kind of leverage that will be especially valuable for literary scholars, but there are many other promising methods to explore: topic modeling, social network analysis, and geocoding, for instance.[30] Moreover, a quick survey of work by other distant readers will turn up dozens of literary topics not addressed in these pages at all—formal questions about plot and suspense or social questions about ethnicity and race.[31] Improvements in natural language processing will soon open up a wider range of questions about character.[32]

In short, I am confident that this volume has come nowhere

29. Hoyt Long and Richard Jean So, "Turbulent Flow: A Computational Model of World Literature," *Modern Language Quarterly* 77, no. 3 (2016): 345–67.

30. For the potential of geocoding, see especially Matthew Wilkens, "The Geographic Imagination of Civil War Era American Fiction," *American Literary History* 25, no. 4 (2013): 803–40. For reflection on topic modeling, see Rachel Sagner Buurma, "The Fictionality of Topic Modeling: Machine Reading Anthony Trollope's Barsetshire Series," *Big Data and Society*, December 1, 2015, http://journals.sagepub.com/doi/full/10 .1177/2053951715610591.

31. For an attempt to model plot, see Archer and Jockers, *Bestseller Code*, 73–111. For race, see Richard Jean So, Hoyt Long, and Yuancheng Zhu, "The Dark Code: Computation, Race, and the History of White-Black Literary Relations, 1880–2000" (forthcoming).

32. Andrew Piper has already shown, for instance, how a character trait like introversion can intersect with physical features of an imagined world, like windows. Piper, *Enumerations*, 138–43.

near exhausting the potential of its subject. There are many historical patterns too large to be explored through the narrow aperture of a single reader's memory. New methods are now revealing some of those patterns, but the most important thing they have revealed is that we never grasped the outlines of the past as well as we supposed. To return to the metaphor in my title: we may have acquired enough altitude now to see that the horizon of literature is curved. But that discovery should only remind us how little we understand literary history as a whole.

Acknowledgments

We say "The Rime of the Ancient Mariner" was written by S. T. Coleridge, although his friend William Wordsworth really came up with the albatross idea. This book was written by "me" in somewhat the same sense. Much of chapter 3 was originally a collaboration with Jordan Sellers, later enlarged by further collaboration with Sabrina Lee, Jessica Mercado, and Kyle R. Johnston. Much of chapter 4 first appeared as a collaboration with David Bamman and Sabrina Lee; that chapter wouldn't exist at all without David's software. But both chapters have been transformed significantly by subsequent work, and my original collaborators should not be held responsible for errors in my changes and additions.

To get the data in the first place, I worked with HathiTrust Research Center, where Loretta Auvil, Shawn Ballard, Boris Capitanu, Eleanor Dickson, Stephen J. Downie, Yu Ma, and Peter Organisciak guided me to the right pages in sixteen million volumes. Other texts were drawn from the Chicago Novel Corpus, organized by Hoyt Long, Richard Jean So, and Teddy Roland. Further guidance came from John Unsworth, Alan G. Thomas, George Roupe, Allen Riddell, David Mimno, Sharon Marcus, Laura Mandell, Heather K. Love, Alan Liu, Matthew

Jockers, Ryan Heuser, Harriett Green, Andrew Goldstone, and James F. English.

I thank the editors of *Modern Language Quarterly* and *Cultural Analytics* for permission to reprint portions of chapters 2, 3, and 4 that first appeared in their publications.[1] But since data sets keep growing and models keep improving, readers will notice differences and additions in all three chapters.

Funding for the project came from the National Endowment for the Humanities, the American Council of Learned Societies, the Andrew W. Mellon Foundation, the National Center for Supercomputing Applications, the Center for Advanced Study at the University of Illinois, and especially from the NovelTM project, funded by Canada's Social Sciences and Humanities Research Council and directed by Andrew Piper. My views and findings do not necessarily reflect those of the funding agencies.

Finally, a short book that pretends to cover several disciplines and three hundred years depends heavily on the advice of friends who tell you to read or quote something so you don't make a fool of yourself. There are too many of those to list, but Eleanor Courtemanche's advice about the history of the novel and literary theory informed the whole project, and approximately 30% of the books cited were borrowed from her.

1. In particular, the first half of chapter 3 originally appeared as Ted Underwood and Jordan Sellers, "The Longue Durée of Literary Prestige," *MLQ* 77, no. 3 (2016): 321–44. Parts of chapter 2 appeared as Ted Underwood, "The Life Cycles of Genres," *Cultural Analytics*, May 23, 2016, http://culturalanalytics.org/2016/05/the-life-cycles-of-genres/. Parts of chapter 4 appeared as Ted Underwood, David Bamman, and Sabrina Lee, "The Transformation of Gender in English-Language Fiction," *Cultural Analytics*, February 13, 2018, http://culturalanalytics.org/2018/02/the-transformation-of-gender-in-english-language-fiction/.

Appendix A: Data

In the humanities, writers ordinarily support their arguments with a list of sources so readers can look up the original texts. But a quantitative argument based on hundreds of thousands of volumes needs more than a list of sources: it needs to enable readers to check the math. To make that possible, I have provided the data and code used for this argument in an online repository.[1] Readers are encouraged to download the repository and examine the steps of the analysis. Readers familiar with the Python programming language can tinker with my code and discover how much that alters my results.

I cannot provide the original text of all the books used here; copyright law prevents it. But the controversial part of analysis usually begins after words have been counted, so the data I can legally provide—lists of word frequencies associated with each volume or fictional character—should allow intrepid readers to retrace the most debatable parts of the argument. An argument that can be retraced in this manner is "reproducible."

In addition to providing word counts for volumes, I have associated most titles with a volume identifier in HathiTrust Dig-

1. Underwood, "Data and Code to Support *Distant Horizons*," Zenodo, last modified March 25, 2018, http://doi.org/10.5281/zenodo.1206317.

ital Library. Readers who want to rebuild the argument from scratch can retrieve the raw texts from HathiTrust and do the word counting themselves (or have the word counting done inside a secure data capsule, for works in copyright). Of course, if you really want to test my arguments rigorously, it might be better not to use the same set of books. For a more severe test, you could create your own independent sample of volumes, and ask whether my generalizations hold true in that sample as well. If my conclusions hold true in different subsets of the literary past, they are not just reproducible but "replicable." I have already tried this test myself, where possible; for instance, chapters 2 and 4 mention that I have checked results both against HathiTrust and against an alternate sample of works collected at the Chicago Text Lab. But this is still a relatively young field. We will only discover the limits of our knowledge by rigorously testing it in many different ways.

It may surprise some readers that I have deferred a detailed discussion of data to the end of this book. Debates about distant reading have often centered on controversy about the construction of data. But I believe this is now a residual controversy, hanging on beyond the period when it made sense. It has lingered because the term *distant reading* is still defined, for many scholars, by the polemical context that surrounded it in the year 2000, when it seemed to be the culmination of a long argument over the canon. The pathos of a title like Franco Moretti's "Slaughterhouse of Literature" came from the implication that existing recovery projects had been inadequate. Of course, Moretti also said that his goal was not simply to expand coverage. The real point was rather a new form of comparative analysis made possible by expansion. "Slaughterhouse," for instance, contrasts Arthur Conan Doyle to his contemporary rivals.[2] But in the polemical context of the canon wars, this emphasis on comparison was not the part of Moretti's argument that got heard; what got heard

2. Moretti, "Slaughterhouse," 207–8.

instead was a forceful claim that critics' bookshelves had to be replaced by the whole library.

A claim of that kind was guaranteed to annoy several different audiences. In defense of canonical works, many scholars replied that widely discussed books may be more important than others: surely a representative sample of the past would assign different weight to different volumes?[3] Scholars interested in minority literatures replied that historical injustices have left some groups underrepresented in libraries. An indiscriminately comprehensive collection of books might continue to allow those voices to be drowned out.[4] Finally, book historians perceived Moretti's discussion of the slaughterhouse as a simplified version of their own long-standing argument that criticism of great works ignores literary circulation. This is not a problem that can be solved simply by multiplying titles. As Katherine Bode has explained, a collection dated by first publication will never capture the temporality of reading practices, which are free to range over the whole past.[5]

All of this is true. Every sampling method has limitations, and these are the limitations of a sample that tries to include one copy of every title, dated by first publication. If *distant reading* meant a belief that such samples are the only valid way to represent the past, then these limitations would constitute an argument against distant reading. But quantitative inquiry about literary history has never, in reality, limited itself to a single representation of the past. Sometimes distant readers take the whole library as it stands, but often we select subsets, in order to contrast them. Chapters 2 and 3 of this book, for instance, work with subsets targeted at specific questions about genre and prestige. Where books are missing from digital libraries, distant readers often fill in the gaps. Maryemma Graham, Hoyt Long, and Richard So

3. Rosen, "Combining Close and Distant.".

4. Ryan Cordell, "What Has the Digital Meant to American Periodicals Scholarship?," *American Periodicals: A Journal of History and Criticism* 26, no. 1 (2016): 2–7.

5. Katherine Bode, "The Equivalence of 'Close' and 'Distant' Reading; or, Toward a New Object for Data-Rich Literary History," *MLQ* 78, no. 1 (2017): 77–106.

have digitized hundreds of books by African American writers in order to address one such gap. Sometimes distant readers date books by first publication in order to pose questions about the history of literary production. But just as often we leave reprints in the collection in order to acknowledge the durability of widely read works. Sometimes we consult library circulation records or compare books reviewed in different social locations in order to focus specifically on reception.[6]

In short, large-scale literary research is necessarily comparative. Distant readers often explicitly test their claims against several different samples of the literary past, as I have done for instance in the second half of chapter 4. But even when an argument relies on a single data set, quantitative researchers implicitly understand its claims as part of a larger conversation, organized by a goal of replicability that entails comparisons between different kinds of samples. Critiques of distant reading that argue for or against a particular sampling strategy miss their target by misunderstanding the shape of this conversation. I am responding to those critiques in an appendix because I think they are well-intentioned red herrings.

Why have critics of distant reading overlooked its comparative dimension and portrayed different collections of books instead as competing alternatives? I don't doubt that some of Moretti's more polemical sentences played a role in provoking this response. But more broadly, this is an assumption we inherit from the last few decades of the twentieth century. The critical interventions of that period did commonly aim to displace one object of study with another, presented as better mirroring social reality. When canons were at issue, the struggle to define a single representative list was motivated by the limitations of space that force anthologies and syllabi to distill the past down to a single

---

6. For a distant reading of library circulation records, see Lynne Tatlock, Matt Erlin, Douglas Knox, and Stephen Pentecost, "Crossing Over: Gendered Reading Formations at the Muncie Public Library, 1891–1902," *Cultural Analytics*, March 22, 2018, http://culturalanalytics.org/2018/03/crossing-over-gendered-reading-formations-at-the-muncie-public-library-1891-1902/.

set of texts.[7] In such a confined space, the games critics play are genuinely zero-sum in character: new canons can come into being only by displacing old ones.

Moretti's turn-of-the-century articles sometimes follow the same rules and propose to replace the canon with a new object of study. That move turned out to be an effective way to focus literary scholars' attention. But it was also an anomaly in the larger history of quantitative literary study, which has not usually centered on debates about the canon. Once researchers have created digital collections of several thousand titles, it becomes unnecessary to decide on a single representation of the past, since digital collections are easy to subdivide and rebalance. A collection of this sort is analogous to a library, not to a syllabus or anthology: it doesn't replace one version of the past with another but provides an enlarged repertoire of options. Instead of arguing about samples as if they were competing canons, we can adopt a relational mode of reasoning about literary history, akin to the methods of social science.

Social scientists don't, after all, begin by stabilizing a single list of people who will count as a representative sample for all future inquiry. They assume that there are far too many questions about human behavior for any one sample to suffice. Some questions will need detailed evidence about a small group of people who are all the same age; other questions will need a broad sample ranging across ages, nations, and socioeconomic backgrounds. Although framed differently, the results of those two studies may eventually interlock and become mutually illuminating. Similarly, in literary study, researchers who focus on reception may want a sample that emphasizes popular works and includes every edition of them. Researchers interested in literary production may need a broader sample limited to first editions. There is no need for scholars to decide which of those samples more

---

7. The connection between the canon and the syllabus is explored in John Guillory, *Cultural Capital: The Problem of Literary Canon Formation* (Chicago: University of Chicago Press, 1993), 29–38.

correctly represents the past. Instead, we can compare them and explore the differences. As Benjamin Schmidt has expressed this: the goal is not to construct an unbiased sample but to understand each "source *through* its biases."[8]

Since I approach sampling in this pluralistic way, the data underpinning this study has not been organized around a single master list of representative books. Instead, each chapter develops a different sample, to address a different question. Of course, it would be a lot of work for researchers to construct new samples completely from scratch for every project. So, in practice, digital libraries provide an important resource, allowing researchers to construct different samples by subdividing a larger collection. In pursuing work of this kind, we don't necessarily have to decide whether libraries are correctly balanced. We can rebalance our samples as needed. But we do have to spend some time thinking about the outer limits of the collection. In this book, for instance, the texts I use are mostly drawn from HathiTrust Digital Library. While a sixteen-million-volume collection is not severely confining, it does have limits worth thinking about, since (as we saw in chapter 4) the library includes only about half the fiction titles mentioned in *Publishers Weekly*. More importantly, coverage varies across time; it becomes distinctly less complete as we move forward to the twentieth century, especially in the period beyond 1923. As we look at changes across a long timeline, we should remain aware that we're looking at a sample of varying social breadth.

But problems like this one are not likely to be solved by constructing a correctly balanced sample. There will always be good arguments for representing the past in different ways. For instance, one could argue that it is actually appropriate to study a sample that represents 60% of nineteenth-century literary production but only about 20% of titles published in the twentieth

8. Benjamin Schmidt, "Reading Digital Sources: A Case Study from Ship's Logs," *Sapping Attention*, November 15, 2012, http://sappingattention.blogspot.com/2012/11 /reading-digital-sources-case-study-in.html.

century, because the long tail of publishing becomes vastly longer over time, without becoming vastly more important. If we take that view, the existing balance in libraries might be roughly the balance we want. The solution to these dilemmas is not to stabilize a single sample, in any event, but to try different possibilities and compare them. In doing so, we will learn how much our results are transformed by the variables at issue.

Even if we were restricted to HathiTrust, we could begin to pose questions about the world outside its limits by comparing different subsets of the library. For instance, if a particular trend line flattened out in the obscurest reaches of HathiTrust, we might infer that it will look even flatter in the even-more-obscure volumes never acquired by librarians. But it is also possible to go outside HathiTrust for comparative touchstones. In this book, I have often consulted a collection of novels at the Chicago Text Lab, organized by Hoyt Long and Richard So; almost half the volumes in their collection are missing from my HathiTrust sample. For twentieth-century questions, I have occasionally consulted *Publishers Weekly*.

Other distant readers have been similarly cautious, comparing various samples of the literary field—canonical or obscure, including reprints or excluding them.[9] Caution of this kind will always remain necessary. But we should also be frank about the size of the difference it has made so far. Cautious comparison of different sampling strategies has almost never changed distant readers' conclusions about century-spanning trends.

"Century-spanning" is the key phrase in that sentence. If we set out to create a complete and balanced picture of a single decade, the list of volumes we choose will matter a great deal. But I have argued throughout this book that the salient strength of distant reading is to reveal arcs of change across long timelines. For that goal, many different samples are often equally appropriate. Trends that shape two hundred years of literary history are usually reflected in every part of the literary field. Whether

9. Algee-Hewitt et al., "Canon/Archive."

we focus on prominent works or obscure ones, the same trends become visible.

To be sure, there are also interesting things we can learn by comparing samples. For instance, researchers at both Illinois and Stanford have noticed that canonical works are commonly fifteen or twenty years ahead of the curve.[10] That's a telling detail, likely to repay further investigation; chapter 3 of this volume can be understood as an attempt to unpack the implications. But a difference of fifteen years between more and less prominent writers doesn't undermine our initial observation that, for instance, literary production as a whole has been moving toward concrete description for two centuries. That remains true, whichever sample we choose.

I suspect critics of distant reading have spent most of their energy on otiose debates about corpus construction because it's the part of this project literary scholars are best equipped to critique. Debates about representativeness have long been central to literary study. But statistical inferences are almost unknown, and we're not yet comfortable testing them. Both of these dimensions of an argument deserve scrutiny, to be sure. But I suspect our anxieties have been misallocated between them. Literary scholars are not trained to think skeptically about the magnitude of evidence; in fact, our discipline positively celebrates insightful guesses founded on tiny details. So when distant readers slip into dubious territory, I find we usually go wrong by overselling an arbitrary metric or overreading one intriguing (and probably random) wobble in a trend line. By contrast, I haven't yet seen a case where an argument about century-spanning trends was undermined by the researcher's initial choice of books. Literary scholars tend to be cautious enough about that part of their argument.

So, while we continue to think cautiously about sampling and data construction, I would recommend allocating a bit more anxiety to the disciplinary blind spots that wreck our arguments

10. Algee-Hewitt et al., "Canon/Archive," 2.

more often. Researchers should share code, report effect sizes, and measure uncertainty where possible. In this book, for instance, effect sizes have been measured as correlation coefficients or model accuracies; uncertainty has been measured both through resampling and by testing different interpretive assumptions. I have also spent much of this book arguing that supervised models should be preferred to arbitrary measurements that aim to "operationalize" a concept.[11] In practice, I think these methodological questions make a bigger difference than the questions about data construction critics have tended to dwell on.

That being said, the next stage of research in distant reading probably does involve a richer and more careful sort of sampling. We will want to gather more social evidence, especially about reception, so we can subdivide samples more carefully, describe shorter timelines more richly, and in some cases move toward causal explanation of literary change. This volume takes a few tentative steps in that direction, but there is a great deal more to be done. At the same time, we can expand our samples of literature by filling gaps, improving texts, and correcting dates. Our existing digital libraries are undeniably imperfect. Optical transcription of eighteenth-century books is so bad that it remains hard to do certain kinds of research in the period. Pulp magazines are not well covered, and more generally, it is not easy to extract a single story or article from a serial. Languages other than English are not always well served; within English literature, ethnic minorities need richer representation. Metadata are imperfect: in this book I have usually limited my collection to the earliest copy of each title, but in chapters 1 and 4, working with hundreds of thousands of volumes, I have not rigorously dated everything by first publication. (Since chapters 2 and 3 covered only a few thousand volumes, I was able to date volumes manually, and more accurately.)

---

11. Here I am resisting the argument offered by Franco Moretti, "'Operationalizing': or, The Function of Measurement in Modern Literary Theory," Stanford Literary Lab Pamphlet 6, December 2013, https://litlab.stanford.edu/LiteraryLabPamphlet6.pdf.

In fact, it is still difficult to extract "fiction" or "poetry" from a digital library at all. A human reader knows to flip past the introductory biography of Jane Austen and start with "It is a truth universally acknowledged. . . ." A human reader also knows to skip page numbers, running heads, illustrations, and advertisements. But a computer doesn't do any of that automatically. Even worse, a computer doesn't necessarily know which books count as fiction to begin with. Evidence about genre is often left out of digital records, and the boundaries of fiction are in any case blurry. We may underestimate this blurriness, because the most ambiguous material doesn't often get taught in literature classrooms. But library shelves are full of lightly fictionalized biographies and histories, quasi-autobiographical travel writing, and the like.

So when I write "the texts in this book are mostly drawn from HathiTrust," I am describing a messy process that stretched over several years. In collaboration with graduate students and staff at HathiTrust Research Center, I had to first identify volumes of poetry and fiction (algorithmically, because metadata are sparse) and then separate the poetry or fictional text from tables of contents, ads, running heads, and prefaces.[12] Whenever possible, I also corrected optical transcription errors (so *hiftory* becomes *history*) and normalized spelling to modern British practice (so *color* becomes *colour*, *physick* becomes *physic*, and *to-day* becomes *today*).

However, I am confident that there are still thousands of errors in my data, both in the texts and in the metadata. I know, for instance, that a small fraction of books I have listed as fiction are really biographies or travel writing. In chapters where I work with a few thousand volumes (2 and 3), I can groom the metadata manually to a fairly high standard, but it isn't possible to do that for the hundreds of thousands of books used in chapters 1 and 4. Research on that scale is about measuring error, not eliminating it.

12. Ted Underwood, "Understanding Genre in a Collection of a Million Volumes: Interim Report," figshare, 2014, https://doi.org/10.6084/m9.figshare.1281251.v1.

In particular, I have measured variations in the error rate. This book never tries to describe a single year with absolute precision; it usually describes a pattern of change across decades or centuries. So an error rate of 5% or 10% is often tolerable, as long as the rate doesn't vary enough across the timeline to have created the trends I am describing. Information about levels of error in data and metadata has been stored with the data online; I have tried to make claims that are consistent with observed levels of error.

However, readers need not take my assurances on faith. This book makes extraordinary claims, which will need to be tested from many angles. The point of sharing code and data is to help readers test those claims in a consequential way. Since I have shared the code I used to draw inferences, a reader who discovers errors in my data has been empowered to say exactly how much those errors change my conclusions. Of course, this also raises the bar for significant criticism. Having gone to great lengths to make it possible for skeptics to prove me wrong, I think it is fair to expect that they actually do so. When an author has shared code and voluminous data, it is no longer enough to draw up a list of scattered errors and omissions that might—who knows?—have altered the book's conclusions. Armed with the author's code, a critic who finds a genuinely consequential oversight should be able to take the next step and demonstrate that it was in fact consequential.

I fully expect that to happen: this book will turn out to be wrong on some topics. The goal of experimental inquiry is not to get everything right the first time but to advance knowledge in a way that invites further testing and refinement. In fact, if long arcs of literary change are as hard to perceive as I have claimed, then I ought to have misunderstood them in some way.

I also know that the data I have shared will need to be improved by other hands. In writing this book, I was divided between two goals. I wanted to work with publicly available texts and build data sets that could be borrowed by other researchers. But I was also concerned not to repeat an error that I think has stalled quantitative scholarship in the past: a preoccupation with precision so meticulous that researchers end up correcting texts, perfecting markup, and in general laying groundwork for an indefinite future instead of actually making an impact on the field of literary history. So, while I spent years correcting this data, I stopped as soon as it became good enough to answer the broad questions about change envisioned in this book. Scholars who want to address different questions may need to further enrich and correct my data sets or develop their own.

I am not sure that I struck the right compromise between the imperatives to produce data for others and to advance my own immediate thesis. But I do feel confident that a compromise of some kind is necessary. We need to keep improving digital collections. But in order to motivate that work, we also need to show that our collections, as they stand, are already capable of addressing important questions.

Appendix B: Methods

Beyond simply explaining the methods used in this book, this appendix presents choices about statistical modeling as decisions that imply an interpretation of recent intellectual history. It may be an understatement to say that this view of statistics is not yet common in the humanities. More often, scholars imagine quantitative methods as stable tools and skills that would at best be "applied" to humanistic material. The value of applying them might be debatable, but the methods themselves are understood to be a settled question. In fact, concerns about the use of numbers in the humanities have emerged in large part from a perception that numbers are used to settle questions—closing down debate and collapsing interpretation into an appearance of objectivity.[1]

But theories of quantitative reasoning are not really much more settled than literary scholars' own theories of interpretation. The history of statistics is a lively part of intellectual history; it includes theoretical controversies (like the Bayesian/frequentist debate) that have stretched across several centuries, as well as

---

1. Some writers, while aware that statistics is itself a sophisticated mode of reasoning, are concerned that digital humanists will appropriate it in a simplified form. See Drucker, "Humanistic Theory and Digital Scholarship."

recent questions (for instance, about the trade-off between prediction and interpretation) that are bound up with conflict over the social role of machine learning.[2] As I learn more about this history and try to communicate it to scholars familiar with humanistic tradition, I am often reminded of science fiction stories about problems of translation between two equally advanced civilizations working on similar problems in incommensurable languages.

If I can extend that stretched metaphor even further, we might think specifically of a story that acknowledges the limits of light-speed communication, so that each civilization is really observing and communicating with a hundred-year-old version of the other. A similar lag is responsible for many misunderstandings between disciplines. When scientists talk to literary scholars, they often pitch their remarks for an audience attached to Romantic theories of the imagination. Literary scholars, conversely, imagine they are negotiating with nineteenth-century determinists. Efforts to improve communication between these two cultures perhaps need to begin by recapitulating their history for each other. Scientists could use a season-opening recap like "Previously, on literary theory, historical materialism reframed the creativity plot line as a story about social change." Literary historians, conversely, could use a recap covering debates about probability.

I cannot fit that whole story into the margins of a book about literary history. But I should at least begin by observing that the point of numbers in social science is not to impose determinism but to acknowledge uncertainty. For instance, we may think we glimpse patterns and trends in literary history. But patterns in human history are rarely deterministic laws. So to achieve an appropriate interpretive skepticism, we need a way of representing patterns that also acknowledges unexplained variation in the

2. For an accessible history of debate about Bayesian statistics, see Sharon Bertsch McGrayne, *The Theory That Would Not Die: How Bayes' Rule Cracked the Enigma Code, Hunted Down Russian Submarines, and Emerged Triumphant from Two Centuries of Controversy* (New Haven, CT: Yale University Press, 2012).

evidence. Statistical models provide that flexible representation. They allow us to reason about the strength of a given hypothesis relative to other variation our hypothesis doesn't explain. Tinkering with a model can also allow us to ask how robustly a hypothesis would hold up under alternate interpretive assumptions.

Up to this point, our season-opening recap works fairly well, avoiding technical mystification to communicate statistical reasoning instead as a transparent move in an interpretive argument.[3] The bump in the road for this story is that statistical models of a classic, simple kind with two or three variables never became very useful for humanists. It is not an accident that our disciplines mostly ignored statistics in the twentieth century. At that point in their history, statisticians genuinely couldn't do much to help us. Sociologists might construct simple models that related, say, a child's income to the income of the parent, plus some amount of unexplained variance. But humanists don't tend to work with simple measures of inequality expressed in a neat table. We work with novels, photographs, pamphlets, and symphonies—things that do not reduce easily to two or three variables.

So the methods used in this book are often more complex. To be sure, where quantitative methods can be kept simple, I believe in keeping them simple. Sometimes a single variable is enough: we can just count the number of books or measure the frequency of a word. But as I explained in chapter 1, isolated linguistic variables are often hard to interpret because their meaning is not clear without social context. A model that connects linguistic variables to social ones can develop a stronger web of hermeneutic connections.

However, it was hard to build those connections until late in the twentieth century, when it became possible to build models with thousands of variables. That delay is why literary scholars now find themselves going back to recapitulate a hundred-odd years of the history of quantitative disciplines: statistics didn't be-

3. A fuller presentation of this approach to statistics can be found in Robert P. Abelson, *Statistics as Principled Argument* (New York: Psychology Press, 1995), xi–16.

come useful for us until rather late in the game. A brief appendix cannot retrace this whole story. We have to jump forward to the last forty years or so, when statistical models started to become useful for humanists, as they became more capable of grappling with unstructured humanistic evidence.

Of course, even today, no mathematical model can perfectly capture a symphony or a novel. But in practice (as this whole book has shown) we can identify broad patterns in literary history if we represent each work as a data point characterized by several thousand variables. This was slow to happen, however, because models on that scale confront some fundamental obstacles. Choosing variables is not the crux of the problem: the point of using thousands of variables is partly that we may not know which ones are most important. Simple omnivorous representations of text are often sufficient: for instance, we can just treat the frequency of each word as a variable. The trickier challenge lay in the sheer complexity of these models. The solution lay partly in the personal computer, which made it possible to juggle several thousand variables casually on a desktop. But it also depended on new theories about the purpose of modeling.

In the middle of the twentieth century, models that used thousands of variables were limited not just by computing power but by the epistemological problem of false precision. A model with more variables than data points can, in effect, simply memorize every point. The model may appear to explain the evidence perfectly, but since it hasn't learned anything generalizable, it won't explain new evidence well at all. We say that a model of this sort has "overfit" a particular sample. In twentieth-century social science, the solution to overfitting was often to handpick a small number of important variables; this was understood as specifying an appropriately "parsimonious" model. With fewer variables, a model would be unable to overfit the sample. But this solution rarely works well for unstructured text, since it isn't clear which five or ten words one would pick in advance as symptoms of, say, literary prestige.

Toward the end of the twentieth century, researchers in statistics and machine learning came up with a variety of practical tricks that permitted modeling more complex data. One solution is to constrain model complexity mathematically: one might think of this as deliberately adding "fuzziness" to a model, in order to force it to learn a generalized representation instead of memorizing the examples.[4] But in order to decide how much fuzziness to add, we also need a better metric of success than the model's closeness of fit to the original training set. Maximizing fit would always encourage us to overfit the evidence. So researchers got in the habit of testing models by asking them to make predictions about a sample other than the sample originally used to train the model. By making it possible to model complex data without false precision, this strategy made statistical models applicable not only to tables with five or ten variables but to less structured kinds of evidence, like images and text. The diffusion of quantitative methods in the humanities has thus depended on a deeper advance in our understanding of what it means to generalize about evidence. At bottom, in fact, it involves a new theory of learning.[5]

I initially described strategies for avoiding overfitting as a collection of "practical tricks," which is more or less how they arose. But as Leo Breiman pointed out in a classic article, strategies of this kind eventually imply a fundamentally different conception of a model's purpose. When researchers were restricted to a small set of variables, they could imagine that the process of selecting variables for a model was also crafting a parsimonious description of the phenomenon being modeled (and perhaps

---

4. In the statistical literature, this is called shrinkage, regularization, or biased estimation, not "adding fuzziness." One historically important contribution was Arthur E. Hoerl and Robert W. Kennard, "Ridge Regression: Biased Estimation for Nonorthogonal Problems," *Technometrics* 12, no. 1 (1970): 55–67.

5. The core of this theory is the concept of a trade-off between bias and variance. An accessible explanation can be found in Scott Fortmann-Roe, "Understanding the Bias-Variance Tradeoff," June 2012, http://scott.fortmann-roe.com/docs/BiasVariance .html. For a magisterial treatment, see Trevor Hastie, Robert Tibshirani, and Jerome Friedman, *The Elements of Statistical Learning: Data Mining, Inference, and Prediction*, 2nd ed. (New York: Springer, 2017).

even a causal explanation of it). But methods that allow a model to retain hundreds or thousands of variables no longer aim for the kind of parsimony we call "explanation." Instead of envisioning the modeling process as directly fitting and representing a simpler structure underlying the data, it makes more sense to acknowledge that we are selecting a model that makes accurate predictions, without any proof that the inner workings of the model mirror deep structures in the world.[6]

Here we reach a controversial crux in recent intellectual history. Many of the advances of machine learning depend on a systematic agnosticism that effectively restricts itself to prediction, deferring explanatory questions. Some observers are troubled by that agnosticism. Peter Norvig has argued with Noam Chomsky about this, and the idea of a "right to explanation" has recently become prominent in social critiques of machine learning.[7] I won't try to survey this whole conversation; it would require another book. But I do want to push back against a rhetorical turn, common on both sides of this debate, that tends to exaggerate the enigmatic and opaque character of predictive models. Both sides indulge this exaggeration, because it attracts readers with an exciting aura of paradox and danger. Chris Anderson championed machine learning in *Wired*, for instance, by claiming that it made the scientific method obsolete: "Correlation supersedes causation, and science can advance even without coherent models, unified theories, or really any mechanistic explanation at all."[8] That statement hugely exaggerates the consequences of machine learning. The scientific method is not obsolete; predictive models still aspire to coherence; experimental inquiry still needs to be guided by theory. But Anderson's exaggeration has

6. Breiman, "Statistical Modeling."

7. Peter Norvig, "On Chomsky and the Two Cultures of Statistical Learning," 2011, http://norvig.com/chomsky.html; Galit Shmueli, "To Explain or to Predict?," *Statistical Science* 25, no. 3 (2010): 289–310; John Frank Weaver, "Artificial Intelligence Owes You an Explanation," *Slate*, May 8, 2017, http://www.slate.com/articles/technology/future_tense/2017/05/why_artificial_intelligences_should_have_to_explain_their_actions.html.

8. Chris Anderson, "The End of Theory: The Data Deluge Makes the Scientific Method Obsolete," *Wired*, June 23, 2008, https://www.wired.com/2008/06/pb-theory/.

been a very useful target for writers who want to avoid machine learning—even for Franco Moretti, who has used Anderson as a foil to argue for a version of quantitative hermeneutics that detours around machine learning (and indeed, around statistical models in general).[9]

Phrased starkly, as an exclusive choice, the tension between "prediction" and "explanation" may occupy philosophers for a long time. But in the real world, these are rarely exclusive alternatives. Most of the predictive models I encounter in my work as a literary historian are not hard to explain. For instance, it is not difficult to solve the riddle posed by the prominence of *police*, *crime*, and *murder* in a model of detective fiction. Some cutting-edge algorithms (like neural networks) can, admittedly, be difficult to interpret. But scandalized discussion of this problem has expanded far out of proportion to its practical significance. For one thing, few distant readers actually use neural networks. As I'll explain in a moment, time-tested and relatively transparent methods are usually adequate for predictive modeling of text.

More fundamentally, the whole premise of a *choice* between prediction and explanation may be phantasmic in fields like the humanities where we have never possessed simple explanatory models. The debate makes more sense in social science. Psychologists once had (or thought they had) simple mathematical equations that governed human behavior. Now they are being asked to consider models that may be harder to understand but that hold up better in practice when confronted with new data. This leads to a real controversy: Do we seek streamlined explanation or maximize predictive accuracy?[10]

But in the humanities, we have rarely produced streamlined explanations of any kind—and certainly not simple mathematical equations. So it is not entirely clear that "prediction versus explanation" is a real trade-off for us, or a painful choice. In fact, for many humanistic questions, winnowing the variables to iden-

9. Moretti, "Patterns and Interpretation."
10. Yarkoni and Westfall, "Choosing Prediction over Explanation."

tify a few key factors is not even an interesting goal. For instance, it is not especially hard to find the key variable that distinguishes masculine and feminine characters in fiction. Hint: they are described with different pronouns. We don't need a statistical model to explain that linguistic boundary. But when I trained models of gender in chapter 4, I excluded pronouns and other obviously gendered words from the process. The point of those models was not to explain gender or define it parsimoniously, but to trace the implicit associations that surround gendered identities and measure their changing strength over time. For that goal, the diffuse complexity of a predictive model was not a regrettable limitation; it was the whole point. Genre presents a similar problem. It can be easy enough to define, say, detective fiction. But the part of the concept that interests us may be the historically volatile part that evades neat definition. Supervised predictive models are useful here precisely because they avoid parsimonious explanation.

I don't mean to rule out explanation in the humanities. There are certainly situations where humanists need to reduce a phenomenon to a few key variables or even frame a causal hypothesis.[11] But we also have a wide range of other goals. I often encounter arguments about quantitative method that seem to be founded on an implicit hierarchy of cognitive tasks, where mere pattern recognition is easy, prediction may be more interesting, but explanation is the real prize.[12] I don't think that hierarchy holds up well in historical disciplines, since historical patterns are not easy to perceive and it is not safe to assume that they have a single explanation. For specific historical events, we may be able to frame good causal narratives. But across a long timeline, change is likely to involve many factors and feedback loops that have cycled through hundreds of times. Pressing too hastily for streamlined explanation at this scale may lead us toward tautol-

11. For a case where explanatory parsimony is valuable, see Hoyt Long and Richard Jean So, "Turbulent Flow: A Computational Model of World Literature," *MLQ* 77, no. 3 (2016): 345–67.
12. See Dennis Yi Tenen, "Toward a Computational Archaeology of Fictional Space," *New Literary History* 49, no. 1 (2018): 119–47.

ogy or distortion. Quantitative models are often better conceived as aids to interpretation that allow us to detect patterns, measure their strength, and compare different frames of reference.

The technical choices I have made about machine learning are guided by this conception of predictive models as sensors that can measure and compare implicit associations in different periods: a method I have called "perspectival modeling." If I were trying to extract crisp explanations from the models, I might use a simpler algorithm, like naïve Bayes, which can assign each word an immediately interpretable coefficient. That would have allowed me to say confidently how important the word *murder* is to a model of detective fiction. But precise explanations are not my primary goal (for instance, because it isn't surprising that *murder* is important). I am more interested in assessing a model's relative degree of confidence about different books, and naïve Bayes has the disadvantage of not naturally expressing those predictions in a well-calibrated probabilistic way.

On the other hand, if I were really interested in squeezing out every fractional percentage point of accuracy, I might have used support vector machines (SVMs), which are, in theory, the state-of-the-art choice for text classification. But SVMs have a degree of complexity that does start to interfere with my interpretive goals. They are difficult to explain, often need to be tuned rather precisely for particular data sets, and don't naturally produce a simple measure of variable importance.

So the primary workhorse of this book has been regularized logistic regression. This algorithm is widely used for text classification and has an accuracy closely comparable to SVMs. But it also works in an intuitive way that is relatively easy to explain. Most crucially, it excels at calibrating its degree of confidence about different observations, which is a feature I used heavily in the illustrations for chapters 2 and 3.

At its core, a regression algorithm infers a relation between variables. If you see a cloud of data points and draw a straight trend line through the middle, you have performed linear regression. The line defines an expected relationship between the

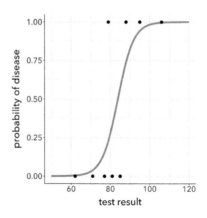

FIGURE B.I. Logistic regression.

horizontal and vertical variables. Logistic regression is used in situations where the response variable (say, the vertical position of each point) is a binary value (either 0 or 1). Suppose, for instance, we are calibrating a medical test, trying to figure out what a given test result implies about the probability of having a disease. We know the test results for a sample of patients and whether they were eventually diagnosed with the disease or not. In this situation, it rarely makes sense to envision the relationship as a straight line. For one thing, a straight line could continue below 0.0 probability and above 1.0, giving some patients 150% probability of having the disease (or a negative 50% probability). That would be meaningless, and also a clue that other predictions are excessively confident. So instead of drawing a line, logistic regression draws a sigmoid curve to estimate the probability of disease associated with different test results.

In figure B.I, we have a regression with only two variables: a single predictor (the test result) and the binary dependent variable (whether the patient was diagnosed with the disease). In the models used in this book, there are usually thousands of predictor variables, so the models themselves cannot be represented in two dimensions (although their predictions can be graphed on a timeline). The models I use also diverge from the thought experiment in figure B.1 because I use "L2-regularized" logistic regression. Regularization is the process I described earlier as "adding fuzziness" to a model. This tends to reduce the model's confidence about the effect of variables; imagine tugging at the ends of the sigmoid curve in figure B.1, so that the curve flattens. A line drawn up (or down) from any actual test result might hit this flatter curve at a vertical point corresponding to 40%–60% probability; in effect we have reduced the confidence of the model. Reducing confidence about variables where our evidence is weak can produce models that are not just more cautious but more accurate about new samples.

The regression algorithm itself is not something a researcher has to write from scratch; I use a standard implementation borrowed from scikit-learn.[13] The more challenging aspects of this method involve selecting documents and variables, tuning regularization, and managing validation. For instance, if we want to model the difference between two genres, it becomes important that examples from both genres are similarly distributed across time. Otherwise we will construct a model that is partly about genre and partly about the chronological difference between two groups of texts. In cross-validating data (training a model successively on one sample of texts and testing it on another), it is important that books by the same author are grouped in the same sample. Otherwise a model can learn to identify detective fiction simply by recognizing Agatha Christie's style. Finally, it is important to tune the regularization constant (the amount of "fuzziness" added to the model). Examining the figures in chapter 2 and chapter 3, a reader may notice that models of genre have volumes clustering near the top and bottom of the image, whereas models of literary prestige have volumes sprinkled more evenly across the space. Fundamentally, this is because prestige is harder to model than genre. So the best models of prestige end

13. Pedregosa et al., "Scikit-Learn: Machine Learning in Python," *JMLR* 12 (2011): 2825–30. Visualizations are produced using Hadley Wickham, *ggplot2: Elegant Graphics for Data Analysis* (New York: Springer, 2009).

up needing a lot of regularization and have relatively low confidence on average.

Details like these require a lot of scrutiny, and I have given them more attention than is immediately visible in these pages. On the other hand, I have tried to minimize questions about variable selection by relying for the most part on a routine strategy where every word (or punctuation mark) is a variable, and the model is based on the *n* words most common in the whole corpus being modeled (after an initial tuning pass to choose *n*). I have given this strategy a few minor tweaks. I often group personal names as a single variable, for instance, as well as place-names and days of the week. I also sometimes include average sentence length and word length as variables. But generally, I try to avoid spending a great deal of effort on feature selection and engineering. For one thing, it doesn't help. I have spent weeks designing systems that assess rhyme and meter, measure conditional entropy in fiction, or count phrases longer than a single word.[14] But these features almost always duplicate information that was already latent in word counts. (One variable that did make a slight difference was the sheer length of a book, but I chose not to include that here because I felt it could muddy certain interpretive inferences.) Moreover, problem-specific tinkering can lead to overfitting, and I suspect it misunderstands the purpose of machine learning in a historical discipline.

Maximizing the accuracy of models is not, in itself, a goal of historical research. The goal is always historical insight. We care about maximizing accuracy only because we want to be confident that we are not leaving evidence on the table. Every model should have a fair chance to be as accurate as possible given the evidence so we can compare models in a meaningful way. But when the differences between models are clearly bigger than any

14. Having attempted to reproduce the result, so far without success, I am tentatively skeptical about the importance attributed to conditional entropy in Algee-Hewitt et al., "Canon/Archive."

likely improvement through tuning, there is no longer much reason to tune.

In the future, as stronger algorithms become available, researchers will have to keep revisiting these methodological choices. Statistical machine learning made it possible to pose new questions about literary history; neural approaches to natural language will, once again, make new questions possible. But the questions are what matter. Improving the sheer accuracy of a model is important, for cultural historians, only insofar as it leads to new insight.

Of course, historical insight can mean a range of things. As this appendix has shown, methodological choices about modeling rapidly turn into debates about the goals of historical scholarship. In exploring those debates, I have tried to make a case especially for predictive models. Prediction may seem like an odd goal for disciplines that study the past. But the gambit of framing testable predictions has made it possible to model complex literary evidence without false precision. Moreover, predictions are not simply things to test or confirm. Comparing the predictions of different models has allowed this book to explore perspectival differences and historical change. I don't imagine, however, that this is the only way machine learning can contribute to the humanities. The advances that make distant reading exciting are not contained in any single breakthrough; they have emerged, rather, from a quickening conversation between statistical method and humanistic theory, which are increasingly intelligible to each other. If that conversation thrives, literary historians may soon be able to choose from a repertoire of quantitative methods suited to different interpretive goals.

Index

Printed and bound by CPI Group (UK) Ltd, Croydon, CR0 4YY

09/06/2025

14685692-0001